Thanks for.
the fun Madrina

Alice

amrandr@tds.net

The Shop
in
Sandy Bay

ALICE RANDT

authorHOUSE®

AuthorHouse™
1663 Liberty Drive
Bloomington, IN 47403
www.authorhouse.com
Phone: 1 (800) 839-8640

Published by AuthorHouse 01/27/2018

ISBN: 978-1-5462-2664-2 (sc)
ISBN: 978-1-5462-2663-5 (e)

Print information available on the last page.

This book is printed on acid-free paper.

Chapter 1

Rusty left her purse, grabbed the camera, and locked the doors to her SUV, leaving it sit on an empty country road. She put the keys in her pocket and picked her way through the ditch. The driveway to the abandon farm site was overgrown with grass and oozing mud after last night's rain. The sun was out this morning, but it was still better to walk in the wet grass and avoid the slippery gunk. That is what she thought at first. After entering the overgrown grove, pushing branches out of her face and swatting at swarming mosquitoes she decided to walk on her tiptoes through the mud.

The driveway curved to the right, but off to the left she saw the tumbled down barn. This was the weather beaten building she spotted from the road that enticed her to tramp through the wet gooey mess in the first place. She stopped to study the structure, and then continued to walk through the weeds to get a close-up look. Rusty was surprised to see a path, and wondered if wildlife also came this way to seek shelter in the old barn. Holding her camera eye level she began shooting. Kneeling for a different angle, she noted how the sun made the wet leaves glisten and how the rusted tin roof took on a coppery glow.

Thinking she had enough pictures to choose from for her calendar's month of May she turned back to the road.

Rusty owned a consignment shop in downtown Sandy Bay where she sold art's and crafts, souvenirs, and gifts to anyone who'd buy them. Her hobby was calendars. Every year she chose a different theme and made them to sell in her shop. Next years theme would be old buildings.

Stepping high through the tall grass to reach the path, it was her intention to take the muddy driveway back to her car, but she changed her mind. "Hmmmm!" Rusty said to her self, "Self, you're here, you're wet up to your knees, your shoes are caked with mud, and you might as well see where this road leads." So she did!

Following the driveway around the curve an old two story farm house came into view. A big sagging porch hung on the west side of the house. Just ahead of her were two long boards, 3 "thick by 12" wide, lying side by side, she supposed they were used as a walkway leading to a small porch with an entrance into the house. She noted a slanted cellar door on the east side. Moving in for a closer look at it, she saw there were iron hinges on either side of the split double door. A big round iron pull in the middle was the handle. Rusty began snapping pictures.

She continued making her way around the house. In the back there was another door about four feet up but no steps.

Coming around to the sagging porch she was surprised to see it hadn't been finished. It had no floor. She shook her head. When she saw a hammer lying across a board that was haphazardly sprawled across some 2 x 4's, she raised her camera and began shooting more pictures. She couldn't help but smile when she noticed another door from the porch leading into the house. Someone had good intentions, she thought. But that one is useless too.

Smelling apple blossoms she turned around to see an old apple orchard. The ancient knarled trees weren't giving up; the pink blossoms filled the air with perfume.

Curiosity got the best of her! Rusty wasn't one to let an opportunity pass her by. She returned to the front porch and climbed the steps to the only useful access into the house. The door had a window that was covered with a faded floral print curtain. Turning the knob she couldn't believe it when the door opened. It wasn't even locked. After her eyes adjusted to the dark room she noted a black cook stove against the back wall with a box of corn cobs sitting close-by. A white table with a faded, cracked oil cloth sat in front of the window overlooking the cellar door. Behind the door a large sink clung to the wall. A 5 gallon pail rested under it to catch the waste water. An empty white porcelain pail sat on the side with a tin dipper hanging on a nail near-by. A small stained mirror hung next to the dipper. On the right sat a white wooden cupboard, and she could see a couple plates and cups through the glass doors.

Stepping into the room, she peeked into a half open door next to the stove where a cream separator stood. Rusty knew what it was because she had seen one in a museum. Odd, she thought, it looks like the people who lived in this empty house just shut the door and walked away. Maybe, they died and no one was left to clean out the house. She raised her camera and took some more pictures. What a treasure, a peek into the past.

Rusty walked into a small dining room where a large square table dominated the middle of the room. A beautiful pink floral antique lamp hung above the table. After a closer look she could see a light bulb through the dirty lamp chimney. They must have had electricity. A dark oak china cabinet filled with dishes stood in one corner. A floor radio took up space on the wall by the window. Walking across the room she lifted the lid of a crank phonograph that sat in another corner and peered inside; a heavy plastic record sat on the spin wheel. The title read, *A Great Speckled Bird.*

I wonder if whoever owns this place realizes what they have here, it's like a museum. She couldn't believe what she was seeing. Who would walk out and leave all this? She decided yes, they must have died and this place was forgotten.

Through the double windows where ragged curtains hung she could see the saggy, floorless porch. Magazines and old newspapers were stacked under the windows. On the table were tobacco cans, pencils, scratch papers and basically just litter. All the floors were covered with worn linoleum; the only designs left were at the edges of the room.

Turning to the left she entered the living room and stopped short. A bearded man in stripe bib overalls, plaid shirt, with a stripe railroad cap perched crooked on his head, sat sleeping in a wooden rocking chair by the window. Glancing around the room she took in an upright writing desk. The tall bookcase side had a round glass and the desk door hung open creating a writing table. She could see the cubicles inside were filled with envelopes. A black leather and wood sofa sat behind a free standing coal stove and a dark maroon couch hugged the opposite wall. A treadle Singer sewing machine stood open in the corner with a pair of denim bib overalls draped over the top.

Rusty backed slowly out of the room and quietly turned to go. She heard the rocker creak; looking back she saw he was standing.

"Who are you? What are you doing here?" the old man croaked. His eyes were blue, big, round, and startled.

She stammered, "I'm so sorry; I thought this was an abandon house. I'm trespassing. I'm so sorry; she repeated, and literally scampered out of the house banging the door behind her. She ran slipping and sliding through the mud to the safety of her SUV.

Kicking off her shoes and throwing them on the floor of the passenger seat, she jammed the key into the ignition. Gravel flew as she tore down the road toward the highway. It was noon when she turned into the driveway of her tiny house at Lakeside Park. Sitting back behind the wheel, she suddenly felt cold and weak. What ever possessed her to break into that house and frighten that poor old man half to death? Looking around she glad to see things seemed normal in the park. Sighing she got out of the car, grabbing her muddy shoes she hobbled barefoot over the gravel to her house. It was exactly 20 steps from her door to the shower; she shed an article of wet clothes at every step.

Chapter 2

Max followed Rusty to the porch and stood watching as she ran through the weeds and brush. "That's a first" he said out loud.

Taking his watch out of his pocket he noted the time. It was getting on to lunch. He went into the kitchen, took the empty pail, and headed for the well. As he pumped water he stared at the weathered barn.

When the pail was full he lifted it off the spout and set it down on the wooden well cover. He looked at the door of the hay mow. It hung by the top hinge, leaving a gapping hole. The screws on the bottom hinge had rusted away. He hadn't been in the barn for months, there was no need. The cows were long gone, as were Bess and Babe his team of black Percheron draft horses. The only things living in the barn now were the bats and a feral Tom cat.

Max sighed, I'll go up there some day, pull it shut and tie it so it doesn't blow off and hit someone in the head, probably myself!

I wonder how long I'd lay there till someone found me. He thought, it could be a day or a couple weeks. Depending on when it happened. No one stopped by anymore. Who'd care anyway?

Max grew up on the farm he now lives on, working side by side with his dad. They had farmed with horses back then. When he thought back to his childhood it seemed like a dream. Looking around his weed filled yard with the dilapidated buildings, he remembered a time when white Leghorn chickens scratched for bugs and colorful Banty's led their chicks through the grove. He pictured himself a young boy on the empty hayrack, reins in hand, heading toward the barn. His instructions were to guide the team through the wide gate; but instead due to his inexperience he had them trying to climb the barn wall. He could still see his dad running to grab the harness then taking their halters to lead them through the gate.

"Dumb horses," he said under his breath, "They should have known better than to walk into a barn wall."

Max remembered his own son's growing up on this farm. They couldn't wait to move away after high school and he seldom saw them. Since Erma, his wife died about 10 years ago, they didn't even call very often. He sighed again. Picking up the water pail he headed for the house to fix himself a sandwich.

Chapter 3

The phone was ringing when Rusty stepped out of the shower. Wrapping a towel around herself, she searched, found her jeans and grabbed the phone out of her pocket. It was Nona. Nona Baton was a faithful employee who helped run her consignment gift shop. In fact she helped her get the shop up and running.

"Hi Rusty, I know your coming in later today, but I was wondering if you could come in earlier, Rick called and my grandson Jay is in a impromptu play in school at 2 o'clock." Rusty looked at the clock above the refrigerator and said, "Sure Nona, I'll be there in a half an hour."

Scooping up her wet, muddy clothes where she had dropped them, she climbed the steps to the loft. She loved her tiny house, but if one thing was out of place it looked like a disaster area. Opening one of the drawers under the full size bed she chose her undergarments. There were four drawers, a place for everything. It was a good thing she didn't need much. A small closet held what needed to hang. After drying her hair and putting on a touch of make–up, she was out the door. Normally if it was nice she'd walk, but she was in a hurry so she drove the few blocks to the store. Parking behind the shop next to the sign that described her wares, she entered the door that stated *Holly, Wood, and Wine* proprietor Hope Albert. Her dad had pinned the name Rusty on her when she was a toddler because of the color of her hair. The name stuck!

"Hey Nona, it's me." Moving a couple boxes out of the way she said, "It looks like we got some new merchandise."

Nona came to the back, "The Cameron sisters brought some pottery, and the winery delivered another case of assorted wine. I haven't had a chance to open the boxes; it's been pretty busy this morning."

"I've had an adventure myself," said Rusty, "but I'll tell you later, you have to run."

Nona looked at her questioningly and said, "I should be back by 3:30 and I'll find places to display whatever is in these boxes."

Just then the bell rang alerting them to a customer. Rusty went to the front of the store and Nona out the back door.

At first Rusty didn't see anyone, and then spotted a small woman in the corner looking at wood products. Her supply included various shelves, hand and machine carved items, bird houses, and wooden boxes of various sizes.

"May I help you find something or are you browsing?" she asked.

"Just looking for now, do you have larger wooden chests or is this the only size you carry?" The lady held up a dark walnut box with a horse carved into the lid.

"I do have a couple larger in the back that I haven't had room for out front, I'll get them for you."

Rusty returned with a good sized chest made out of cherry wood and a smaller oak chest about 9 X 18 inches.

"Perfect," said the woman reaching for the oak chest. She ran her finger over the top. The cover itself was beautiful. It showed a hand carved wolf sitting regal and independent at the edge of a forest. Jack the elderly craftsman who made the chests was from Plains, a nearby town. He was a true artist. Lifting the lid the woman peered inside, examining the red felt lining with her finger, she said "Yes, I'll take this one."

They moved toward the counter and it was only then that Rusty noticed the woman's limp. Concerned she asked, "Did you hurt your leg?"

"Something like that," the woman answered, her brown eyes took on a guarded look. Her purse hung off her left shoulder, her grey streaked brown hair tumbled across her face as she bent to collect her money. She laid a $100 bill on the counter and turned toward the door.

"Don't you want your change? Your receipt?" Rusty called after her.

Balancing the box on her hip she opened the door, "No need" she called back, letting the door bang shut.

Rusty moved toward the window and saw her get in a green older model Volvo. The man driving sped off before the car door closed and they were gone.

Strange day, she said to herself, and thought again of the man she had surprised that morning. It must be coming up on a full moon.

A van pulled up in front of the store and four young women tumbled out and came into the shop. They were all talking and laughing at once. She knew them; two were sisters and two were sisters in law.

"We are looking for a birthday present for Mom," one said as they each headed in a different direction.

The mom they were talking about worked in the bakery across from the gas station. Rusty listened to their lively banter. They brought a brown braided rug to the till. One of the daughters said with a giggle. "Mom needs a new rug for in front of the sink. She spills a lot." All the girls laughed. "Yes, and it's mostly coffee."

The afternoon wasn't real busy, but it was steady, and she was glad when Nona returned to help.

At 5:10 the last customer left with a set of soup bowls, said to be a wedding gift for a friend. Rusty turned the sign to CLOSED and locked the front door. Nona was already pulling the box of pottery out of the back room. Rusty went back for the unopened case of assorted wines.

"This won't take long to display," Nona commented. Then chuckled, "You should have seen the play the fourth graders put on, they had made puppets out of socks, yarn and buttons. Then they created a play from the book, *Where the Wild Things Are.* The book is based on imagination, and what an imagination the fourth graders have." Nona went on describing the play.

Rusty's mind began to wander; she never did get a chance to tell Nona about her morning, it didn't look like she was going to get a chance to tell her now. She was so excited about Jay's play. It would keep till tomorrow.

The store was soon put in order and Nona left calling good night over her shoulder. Rusty gave the shop a sweeping glance, put on the alarm and locked the back door.

She drove home slowly.

Pulling up in front of her tiny house, she saw her friends and neighbors sitting around chatting and enjoying adult beverages.

"Come join us," Jessie called; the neighbors were gathered next door behind Jessie's house.

"Be right there," Rusty answered unlocking her front door.

"What the heck!" she exclaimed. On her counter sat a vase of a dozen yellow roses. How did they get on her counter? She had locked the door hadn't she? She had just unlocked it or wasn't it really locked! Searching the cupboard and floor for a card or a note she didn't find any, maybe it slid under the couch. It hadn't! No clue to whom they were from, she checked the sliding glass door overlooking the deck. It was locked.

Taking a wine glass from the cupboard, an individual serving bottle of Chardonnay from the refrigerator, Rusty went out to join her neighbors.

Tonight a lively conversation was taking place about of all things, how to have a lively conversation. Her neighbors consist of Glen and Ava who spends five months in Minnesota and seven months in Arizona.

Peg and Jacob is a younger middle-aged couple whose kids have left and they wanted to downsize. Peg still works as a nurse in Plains, and Jacob has a construction company.

Bruce is a retired military bachelor, and Ann who spends summers in Sandy Bay and winters in Texas lives across from Bruce.

Jessie had never married, her and Carol, a widow, are good friends.

Trina works as a bookkeeper for Jacobs Construction Company.

Brad is an Industrial Arts teacher and a coach.

Ernie and Rose are the new comers, moving in early this spring.

Then Rusty, her house was one of the first and she moved in early summer 2011. She was living here when the other houses were being built. The landscaping is fairly new, that was the last project finished. For Rusty it was a step up from her studio apartment. Most of the others had decided long ago to enjoy life rather than to take care of a house and yard. They each live in one of the tiny houses in Lakeside Park.

The road around the Park is shaped like a horseshoe. With the ten tiny houses spaced evenly facing the road. Each house has a driveway for cars. Behind the homes is a grassy commons area. A large pergola sits in the middle, furnished with a lawn table and chairs. A fire pit, a small pond with Koi, and landscaped gardens adorned the lawn. The lake lay to the south, and provided a fish fry for the thirteen residents on Saturday nights. The men seemed to enjoy fishing for the entrée. Being this area of the park is fairly new, the young trees don't provide much shade; the neighbors were squeezed into the shade of Jessie's tiny house.

Rusty waited until the conversation turned to other topics. The men discussed the latest game the Twins had played against the Chicago White Sox. Some of the women were discussing how to stay active with the latest activity tracker.

She then turned to Jessie and asked, "Have you noticed anyone hanging around my house today?"

Jessie shook her head, "I've been gone most of the afternoon, Carol and I went shopping and picked up some groceries. Why?"

"I found a vase of yellow roses setting on my cupboard and I don't know how they got there."

"Ho whooeee! A secret admirer I'd say." Jessie commented, her eyes twinkled and her face crinkled when she pursed her lips.

Rusty smiled back, "But what bothers me is who are they from and how did they get in my house and on my cupboard? I'm pretty sure I locked the door."

"You must have forgotten, otherwise no one would be able to get in. Wasn't there a card?" Jessie continued, "If a florist delivered them, they always attach a card."

"No card that I can find, I've looked." Rusty was bummed. "Beside I've had quite a day."

By now Rusty's conversation had attracted more listeners. She launched into her story of arriving to the deserted farm site to take pictures of the old barn for her 2018 calendar, and finding the old man asleep in his wooden rocker.

"I must have scared ten years off his life, I feel so bad about that. Actually if it hadn't been for his striped overalls and striped railroad cap, he could have been Santa Claus with his fluffy white beard."

"There goes your Christmas present this year," quipped Glen with his Irish accent. He lived a couple houses toward the lake with his wife Ava.

Everyone chuckled; Glen saw humor in most things and had a quick wit.

"Even today in the shop," Rusty continued, "a customer bought a chest about this big," she described the size holding her hands about 18 inches apart. "She gave me the money, didn't wait for change or a receipt, and almost ran out the door! But, what was really strange, the person driving the car barely waited for her to get in before they drove away. She was still shutting the door!"

"That is strange," said Brad a single fellow, who lived just behind her, "you've had quite a day, put on your alarm tonight and we'll all keep an eye out for anything out of sorts."

The neighbors began to disband for the evening and head back to their homes.

It was a comforting thought that her friends were there for her. Everyone looked out for each other, they were like a family.

That night lying in bed, looking through the sky light at the stars, she knew what she had to do. Even though finding the yellow roses bothered her, it didn't compare to scaring that poor old man. She knew she was going back to the farm to talk him.

Chapter 4

W hat was that? Rusty sat straight up in bed, BOOM! CRASH! Lightening flashed lighting up her bedroom, then another boom. Rusty looked at the clock, four AM. She groaned and rolled over, but she felt wide awake. Laying in bed listening to the rain pound the roof, she turned on the lamp and reached for her paper back book and began to read.

The next thing she knew the clock buzzed. Startled awake she shut off the alarm, 7 AM. The rain had stopped. Through her skylight she could see the dark clouds racing overhead. A train whistle blew as it roared through town. Rusty grimaced!

"It sure is a noisy morning, I hate that pierce whistle." She mumbled to herself. By the time she got out of the shower, made her bed and poured a cup of coffee, the sun was peeking out of the clouds. Spreading jam on her toast, she sat down by the counter and eyed the roses. Her mind was blank as she stared at the arrangement and ate her breakfast. Putting the last bite in her mouth, a Russian proverb popped into her head, *Fear a goat from the front, a horse from the back, and a man from all sides.* Where in the heck had those roses come from and how did they get on her counter? Rusty picked them up, opened the sliding glass door to her deck and set them on the patio table. Making sure that all the doors were securely locked and the alarm was on, she took off walking to work.

"Good morning" called Nona. Her car door slammed just as Rusty got the back door of the shop unlocked.

"Morning Nona," answered Rusty. They walked into the shop together. She turned off the security alarm and went to the front to unlock the door and turn on the computer.

Nona stopped at the counter in the back room and took the coffee pot to the sink and filled it with water.

Nona brought them each a cup of coffee, "I'm glad it's Saturday and we close at two o'clock, all that rain we got last night played havoc in the yard. The low spots flooded so I'm going to try to make a trench so the water runs to the driveway and down to the storm drain in the street."

"Maybe being the sun is out it will just sink in and dry up by itself, or call your son Rick let him do the heavy work." Rusty answered.

"I could I suppose, but I hate to bother him, he is so busy." Nona continued. "You were going to tell me something yesterday before I left for the school, and we never did get around to talking about whatever it was. What happened yesterday morning?"

Alice Randt

"Oh Nona, you won't believe my day. Let's unpack some of these boxes as we talk and I'll give you the condensed version."

Nona was quiet as Rusty gave her an account of her photography adventure. Then she told her about the woman who came to the store to buy the wooden chest. When she got to the story about the yellow roses Nona had stopped unpacking and was just sitting listening in awe, her fingers covered her mouth, and she looked intently into Rusty's eyes.

"What are you going to do?" Nona asked.

"I don't know!" Just then the door bell chimed and Rusty left to wait on her customer while Nona unpacked some quilted placemats. The rest of the morning seemed to fly by, shelves were dusted, merchandise rearranged and restocked. Customers came and went, most were tourists who were spending time at the lake.

The last customer left at 2:15 with terry hand towels made to attach to a cupboard or oven door. Rusty had one on her stove; it was handy for wiping wet hands.

"Well," said Nona, "what are you going to do?"

"I think some of our smaller items we should sell for just a dollar or two, like our potholders and letter openers." Rusty answered, "Kids come in looking for gifts for their parents, and just have a couple dollars."

"You know darn well what I meant." Nona abolished.

Rusty smiled, "I knew what you meant, I've decided I'm driving out to the farm and talking to that man."

"Where is this farm anyway? Which road did you take out of town? Maybe I know who lives there."

Rusty thought a minute, and then answered. "I went east on the highway, I think maybe a couple miles, there is this road that angles off to the northeast and I pretty much just stayed on that. I'm not sure how far I went but I crossed over an old cement bridge. I noticed this weather beaten' barn through the trees and thought it was unique. I mean, it didn't really look like a barn with a hip roof. The roof was pointed with two lean-tos, one off to each side. It was different. That is why it caught my eye."

"I think I know where you were, there's a small country church out that way. I played organ for a funeral out there a couple years ago."

"I don't remember seeing a church. But I'll pay closer attention when I drive out again this afternoon."

"Do you think you should? Maybe you could pretend nothing happened."

"No, I need to do this," Rusty responded, She turned the lock on the door and flipped the sign to CLOSED. "I'm going to stop at the bakery and pick up some cookies for a peace offering. I really need to see him; he seems to be living in the last century. I don't think anyone is looking out for him."

"Maybe he doesn't want anyone to look out for him, have you thought of that?"

"That could be true, but I'll find out. He may kick me off his property then I'll leave him alone."

Rusty walked a block to the bakery and picked out some date cookies. Older people seemed to like date cookies, didn't they? She picked out a half dozen chocolate chip too, just in case he didn't like date cookies. Then she walked home to her tiny house.

Sandy Bay was a small town. The whole downtown was about three blocks square. There was a grocery store, bakery, her shop, (Holly, Wood, and Wine) a gas station on the corner, a bar and grill, quilt shop, coffee shop, a liquor store, a hardware store, radio shack, and hair salon. The movie theater was out on the highway.

It didn't take long to walk home; Rusty was a little apprehensive unlocking her door and taking off the alarm. She was relieved to see nothing inside had changed since she had left that morning. Sighing she walked to the sliding glass door and looked out onto the deck. The roses were still on the table.

The weather was nice now, but could get cool later; it was only the end of May. Rusty changed into a pair of jeans and grabbed a sweater anticipating a drop in temperature. She took her camera too; you never know when an opportunity arises and she still needed a couple more summer pictures for her calendar. The winter ones were taken, she'd need to wait until fall colors to take snapshots for the September and October months.

Making sure her doors were securely locked and the alarm was on she headed for her SUV.

Jessie stopped her, "Fish fry tonight down by the lake, and we are eating at six. Can you bring a salad?"

"Sure, no problem, Rusty answered, any special kind of salad?"

"Nope, whatever you want, we'll be about thirteen people if everyone comes."

"OK, see you later." Rusty knew she could stop at the grocery deli and pick up some potato or macaroni salad. She'd decide when she got to the store.

Putting her car in gear and she backed onto the road. Now her mind was on the old man, the farm, and not on the fish fry.

Turning on the radio she dialed in to a country music station, and relaxed, enjoying the ride out to the farm. It was a sunny day; the barn swallows flew from one side of the road to another.

I can't figure out why birds fly so low to the road when God gave them the ability to fly high. I hate it when I hit one, and hate it even worse when I need to pick it out of the grill.

Not being real sure if she remembered where this farm was, she kept an eye out for anything familiar. When she drove over the old concrete bridge she thought she must almost be there. Slowing down and looking to the left she spotted the barn through the trees. It had certainly seen better days. A few hundred feet further she saw the overgrown road. Pulling in she could feel the SUV sinking into the soft mud, quickly putting it in reverse she backed out and parked off the road on the gravel. She picked up the bag of cookies, her camera, and put her keys in her pocket after locking the doors. Taking a deep breath she looked at the muddy, weedy driveway and took the first step.

Making her way through the mud and the weeds, she glanced toward the barn, but then turned to her right. She was watching where she put her feet so she didn't see the man until she reached the board walkway leading up to the house. She looked up and he was sitting on the top step of the porch watching her intently. She stopped walking and stood still, Rusty was the first to speak.

"Um, hi, hello," clearing her throat she continued, "My name is Hope, but everyone calls me Rusty. May I join you?"

The old man seemed to be thinking about it, and then said, "Sure, come on up."

"It was me who barged into your house yesterday," she rattled on holding out the white bakery bag, "I brought a peace offering."

The old man reached for the bag, it was then Rusty noticed a dirty blood stained rag wrapped around his right hand.

"Can I ask you what your name is?"

The old man was balancing the sack on his leg; he looked in the bag, and then answered.

"Just call me Max," he paused and waited. "Would you like to have coffee with these cookies?"

"Sure that would be great."

"Wait here, I'll go heat some."

Rusty obediently sat down on the top step while Max got up, set the sack of cookies down, and went into the house. She occupied her time by looking around. The lawn, if you could call it a lawn, didn't look like it had ever been mowed and was full of weeds. Gazing off into a grove of trees she noticed a small shed. A little farther into the trees, almost hidden by the shed she spotted an outhouse.

Of course, there isn't any running water in the house, you have to go somewhere. She thought.

The door slammed and Max was back with a white coffee mug in each hand. He handed one to Rusty, and sat down beside her on the step. She watched as he clumsily set his cup down on the porch floor, spilling some on his already dirty bandage.

"What kind of cookie would you like, date or chocolate chip? Or," she added, "one of each?"

"You take one first, and then I'll decide."

Rusty chose a date cookie and handed Max the bag. He reached in and took a chocolate chip cookie. They ate in silence.

"What happened to your hand?"

"Cut it!"

"Can I see it?"

Max didn't answer but began untying the rag. His hand was swollen and red, the cut didn't look that deep, but it did look infected. Rusty examined his hand.

"That doesn't look good, did you soak it?"

"Nah, it's nothing."

"What did you cut it on?"

"I was sharpening knives on the old grinder and one slipped."

"When did this happen?"

"A couple days ago, Thursday, I think. Every time I bump my hand starts to bleed."

Rusty didn't really want to tell him what she thought, she had just met him, but that cut had to be cleaned.

Finally she said, "Your hand has to be soaked, will you heat some water? I'm going to walk to my car, I have an old first aid kit that may still hold something useful to clean that cut." Rusty went down the steps, and walked through the mud and weeds to her car.

When she returned with the kit the water was warm, Max poured some out of a chipped porcelain tea kettle into a large bowl.

"Do you have a little soap we can put in the water?" She was thinking dish soap, but he returned with a bar of Fels Napa. Rusty dropped it into the bowl and massaged it till the water became milky. Max sat down on the step, holding the bowl in his lap, he put his hand in the water. They sat in silence.

Max was the first to talk. "Who are you really? Where do you come from? Why did you come here?"

"I make calendars for my shop in Sandy Bay. Driving down this road I saw the barn and wanted a picture for next year's calendar. I just stopped to take a picture. When I saw the house I wanted a picture of that too. I thought it was deserted, I would never have barged in on you, I shouldn't have done that and I'm sorry."

"This is a good peace offering," he answered, holding up the sack, with an almost smile.

Rusty returned the smile, "Let's look at that cut."

Max took his hand out of the bowl, the cut looked cleaner. She opened the first aid kit, took out a worn wash cloth and wiped his hand being careful not to touch the wound. She opened the peroxide,

"This is going to sting," she said as she poured out a capful and applied it to the cut. The peroxide bubbled and sizzled. Rusty blew on his hand trying to make it feel better. When she looked up at Max he was smiling through his white beard and looking very amused.

Digging around in the kit, Rusty picked up a tube of antibiotic ointment carefully applied that to the wound and then covered it with a gauze and bandage.

"There that should help," she said, "can I come back Monday and look at it to see how it's doing?"

"Are you bringing more cookies?"

"Maybe I'll choose something else for coffee." She laughed, packing up her kit; she left the peroxide, ointment, and bandages. "I'm leaving this here, and tomorrow soak your hand in soapy water, clean the cut and put on clean bandages."

"Yes 'em, Miss Rusty." He nodded.

Rusty walked down the boards, and then turned. "I'll see you Monday afternoon Max, I'll need to work in the morning."

Max raised his hand in answer, opened the cookie sack and peered inside, choosing a cookie he grinned at Rusty and took a bite. Then he said through a mouthful of cookie crumbs, "Why don't you use the other driveway, it's not so wet and muddy? Just go to the corner and turn left, it's the first driveway, you'll come in by the garage."

Rusty felt foolish and burst out laughing, "I'll see if I can find it!" Then she turned and left.

Walking back to her SUV she picked up a small dead branch that had fallen out of a tree and broke off a stick. Unlocking her car and opening the door she sat sideways on the seat. Rusty unlaced her shoe and slipped it off. Taking the stick she cleaned the mud off the bottom and laid it upside down on the floor of the passenger's seat. Then she repeated the process with the other one. Turning toward the steering wheel, she shut the door and started the motor. She made a U-turn in the middle of the road and went searching for the other driveway. It wasn't hard to find. Rusty drove to the corner, turned left, and went only a short way when she came to the entrance to the farm. The house wasn't that far from the main road and the driveway led up to a shabby looking garage. Surrounding the garage there stood a tangle of trees, bushes and undergrowth. She didn't notice the garage from the house. Heck, you could barely see the house from the road. She pulled into the driveway and stopped. Before backing out she looked behind her and that is when she spotted a church steeple off in the distance.

On the drive home, Rusty began thinking of the salad she had to bring to the potluck that evening. I'd better go home and make something. She thought. I sure can't go into a store barefoot with muddy feet to buy something out of the

Deli. Glancing at her watch she saw she had a couple hours before gathering at the lake.

Less than a half hour later she left her shoes on the step to be washed, and grabbed a kettle out of the cupboard, added water and then set it on the burner to boil. Before heading to the bathroom to wash her feet, she took the pasta from the cupboard and measured out 2 ½ cups. In the refrigerator she found yellow and red mini bell peppers, a few radishes, celery and some Parmesan cheese.

Mixing together ½ cup of Italian Dressing, ½ cup Mayo, ½ t Garlic Powder, ½ t of Italian Blend Seasoning in a small bowl she saw her water was beginning to boil. She dumped in the shell pasta, stirred it, put the cover on and shut the stove off.

She remembered the roses on the deck, looking out the patio door she saw they were still there looking somewhat wilted.

The phone was ringing when she stepped out of the shower and put on a robe. By the time she found her cell phone it had quit. Oh well! They'll call back if it's important. She didn't recognize the number; someone probably misdialed and got her by mistake.

The pasta was done, so she dumped it in a colander, ran cold water over it and went to get dressed.

The mosquitoes might be out, she thought choosing a light blue slack, instead of Capri's, and a long sleeve plaid blouse. No sense getting eaten alive.

It didn't take long to finish the salad. After she added the onion and Parmesan cheese she did a taste test. "Not bad," she said out loud.

People were coming out of their tiny homes, she heard Brad call to Jessie. Rusty covered the salad, took a wine cooler out of the refrigerator and went out to join them.

Tonight the conversation seemed to be about lying. Of all the dumb things people can do lying is right up there with sky diving and running naked through the street. Not all lies are bad though. If your wife asks you if her butt looks big in those pants, it might be better to say, "No honey, I don't think so." If you agree with her, and say "You might be right dear." You're probably in for a 6 week hospital stay. Everyone seemed to agree in a case like that it's better to lie.

Chapter 5

S unday morning, Nona was getting ready for church. She was the organist at St. Marks Lutheran Church where she had played for many years. Services started at 10:00; she was happy about that, the whole afternoon would be free to work in her gardens. Her son Rick took care of mowing her 1 ½ acre yard, but she did the gardening, it was relaxing. Nona loved that her son and Janet lived close-by; she loved spending time with her grandson Jay. In a couple of years he'd be in junior high school sports and too busy to ride his bike over for cookies.

Wrapping the cord around the handle of her curling iron, she tucked it in the drawer and went down stairs. She sat down at the piano and began running her fingers up and down the keys, playing the scales to exercise her fingers. Before leaving the house she filled her insulated mug with coffee and cut a rice krispy bar to eat in the car on the way to church.

Pulling into the parking lot she saw ladies carrying bowls and cake pans.

"Oh Crap" Her memory was getting bad, she completely forgot about the fundraiser. The potluck luncheon was scheduled for today. She had time before service to help set up the tables.

Taking her purse and music sheets with her, Nona hurried to the church basement. She saw the tables had already been set with centerpieces, cups, glasses and a picture of ice water. There were so many women in the kitchen scurrying around it looked as if they were getting in each others way.

Listening she heard someone say, "No, your cutting the pickles the wrong, slice them the long way."

A couple of ladies back in the corner were discussing how much coffee to put in the pot. One said, "Add a little more grounds, I hate weak coffee."

Someone answered, "Well, it shouldn't be so strong that it eats a hole in the spoon."

Nona turned and headed for the stairs, I'm not getting in the middle of all that. She thought Maybe, I can help later with dishes.

Sitting at the organ she arranged the music and began to play, *"Jesus calls us ore' the Tumult."* That song seemed to fit the tumult taking place downstairs.

After church service Nona didn't stay for lunch, nor did she do the dishes, she was anxious to get home to get her gardens ready for planting. Her mind was on her flowers, as she changed into work clothes. There was the bulb garden where the iris and tulips were beginning to peek through the soil. In fact they were up a few inches already. Her apple trees were dropping their blooms. Where to start?

She walked to the garden shed for her gloves and tools. The door didn't lock; it had a piece of wood holding the door closed. It was a small shed about 4 X 6, but it held all her pots, rakes, shovels, pails and everything else she needed to keep her gardens neat and tidy.

Nona began cleaning around the tulips. Then took a shovel and turned over the dirt where she was planning on putting some marigolds, petunias, and pansies. Pansies were her favorite, with their cute little faces. Last she went to the garage, took out the garden tiller, and pushed it around back to the vegetable garden. The cord reached through the garage window and plugged into a socket. The tiller was electric. The trick was not to run over the cord, and she had done that a couple times or more.

The sun was dropping below the horizon when she finished. She loved her yard and gardens, and her old two story house with the big porch. She had all the convenience of city living, but to her it felt like country.

Nona put her tools away, it was when she was walking back to the house that she looked up and saw the green Volvo parked across the street.

Hmmmmm! I think Rusty said it was a green Volvo that took off before the lady had the car door shut.

She went in the back door, walked through the house and peered through the curtain. A woman had gotten out of the car. Yes, that certainly looks like the lady Rusty described. Nona watched as a black Ford Mustang pulled up behind the Volvo. A man opened the car door of the Ford and walked to the window of the green car; the lady limped over to his car and got into the passenger side.

"My Gosh!" Nona said, "That looks like Rusty's ex-husband William!" She watched as the man in the Volvo handed something to William.

It was then Nona thought about getting a license number, by the time she grabbed a pencil the Volvo was pulling away. She didn't get the number, but there was a sticker on the driver's side of the bumper. She couldn't read that either.

Oh Shoot! A lot of help I am. That can't be William; He died in a boating accident a few years ago. It is because of him Rusty was able to move into one of those tiny houses out by the lake.

Nona put that incident out of her mind. She showered, changed, and made an omelet for herself with some toast. Taking her supper outside she sat on her porch in the twilight enjoying her meal and listening to the birds settling down for the night.

It was after midnight when Nona felt a breeze on her face. She turned over, then heard a flutter of wings and felt the breeze again. She sat up and turned on the lamp, just as a bat flew passed again.

She ducked! And shouted! "Holy Smoly, where did that thing come from?" The bat flew over the dresser then back over the bed, diving and dancing back and forth across the room.

Nona grabbed her robe and ducked out the door. Taking the steps as fast as a 55 year old could, she grabbed her purse and was outside in a minute. Her heart was beating as fast as it could without giving her a heart attack. She looked up and saw her bedroom light was still burning.

I'm not going back to shut it off! Now what am I going to do?

She remembered the Holiday Inn Express out on the highway near the interstate and decided that might be the best place to spend the rest of the night.

She also remembered there were sticky pads in the garage to catch mice. It could work for bats too! Padding out there barefoot she found one. Seeing her garden shoes in the corner, she slipped them on and went back to the house. Opening the door a crack she quickly laid the pad just inside the door. Maybe the bat would fly up against the door and fall down, and stick to the pad.

Driving down the highway toward the interstate Nona contemplated about how it was going to look her walking into the hotel in her nightdress.

At least I grabbed a robe, I'm presentable.

Pulling into a parking spot she said to no one in particular, "The hotel has a lot of cars sitting around the lot. I hope it isn't full."

She took her purse, locked the car doors and walked to the lobby, praying there wouldn't be anyone except the clerk at the desk. There wasn't!

"Can I rent a room for part of the night?" Nona asked. She had thought about asking if she could rent a room by the hour, but considering how she was dressed, it was better not to, she didn't want to spend the night in jail.

"If you have $119 you can." The clerk answered curiously.

She wasn't about to give him an explanation and handed over her credit card. She took the key and went in search of room 136.

In the morning Nona would call her son to get the bat out of the house, but for now she was safe. Surprisingly she slept.

When morning came, she used the hotel phone to call Rick. He couldn't believe she went to the Holiday Inn in the middle of the night in her night dress. In fact he burst out laughing as she related her experience. Nona didn't think it was that funny. Then she called down to the desk to tell them she was leaving, snuck out the back door and around to her car.

Rick pulled into the drive way behind her and got out of his car with a badminton racket ready for battle.

"Hey Mom, your looking chipper this morning," He greeted her with a grin.

"Oh be quiet," Nona answered, then begin to giggle. "It is pretty funny isn't it?" she asked.

"I wouldn't expect any less from you." He replied.

Rick followed her to the door. Nona took off her dirty garden shoes on the porch and Rick did the same. Opening the door the bat flew toward them, Nona backed up so quickly she fell backwards into Rick. He jumped over her and stepped on the sticky pad. When he took another step it pulled his sock off. He turned and looked at his mother sitting on the porch. They didn't see the bat.

Rusty's Sunday was more uneventful. It was a beautiful sunny morning so she had chose to walk the six blocks to and from church. Even though it was lunch time she didn't feel least bit hungry. In fact she felt invigorated. Sunday was the day she caught up on the book work at the store and did her laundry. She changed into Capri's and tee shirt, and headed for the shop. Unlocking the back door and taking off the alarm, she went to the front counter, turned on the computer, then went back to start the coffee pot.

Taking her inventory sheet she walked around the store carefully taking note of the items on her shelves. Writing down what was selling and rearranging items that had been there awhile. She noticed the wooden birdhouses were one of the big sellers, and the pottery needed to be restocked. The supply of embroidered towels and pillowcases had dwindled.

Well, she figured, they make good shower gifts. June is the wedding month.

When she finished her bookwork, she swept the floor, mopped and straightened up the back room. It was 4:00 and the sun was still bright when she locked up the shop and started home. Not hurrying, she strolled, stopping to say a few words to those who were out cleaning up their flower gardens and yards.

A basketball rolled down the driveway, Rusty picked it up, dribbled it a couple of times and aimed it at the basketball hoop attached to the garage. It was a tough call to know who was more surprised, Rusty or the two boys who applauded and whooped when the ball swished through the net.

A dark colored car pulled out of Lakeside Park; she waited until it turned the corner before crossing the street and walking up to her house. The park was quiet. Everyone was either gone or resting indoors. Unlocking the front door she knew she wasn't doing laundry. Instead she picked up her book, a bottle of water, and headed to the lake with a folding chair from the deck.

Chapter 6

Rusty filled her coffee mug and unplugged the coffee pot. Looking through the refrigerator she chose an apple and a jellied doughnut. Locking the door behind her she opened her car door and carefully put her coffee in the cup holder. She picked up an envelope lying on the front passenger seat. There was no name and the envelope wasn't sealed. She took out the paper. The message was printed in capital letters and read, *"YOU ARE ONE SMOKIN' HOT WOMAN!"* Rusty looked around and saw no one. This is weird, she thought feeling confused. Who would do this? It isn't funny!

She couldn't remember if the alarm was on in the house. She went back and unlocked her door. No, she had forgotten to set it. Walking around the corner of her house to the deck, she took the yellow roses that she received three days ago and dumped the water out. Taking them to the end of the park road she threw the vase and the flowers into the dumpster. Getting back to her car, she got in and drove to the shop.

Nona came in just as Rusty got the computer up and running. She went to the front of the shop, turned the sign to OPEN and unlocked the front door.

"Are you walking a little funny Nona?" Rusty asked.

Nona laughed, "Yes, I could be, I bruised my tailbone."

Rusty raised an eyebrow.

"How do you do that?" Nona began making faces trying to raise one eyebrow.

Rusty grinned, "I don't know, and don't change the subject! How did you hurt your tail bone?"

Nona laughed as she related her bat story. By the time she was finished they were both laughing.

"Checking into the Holiday Inn in your night gown, you're lucky they didn't call the police."

"I thought about that too! But this is a small town and we only have one policeman, Booga, and we all know him. If by any chance he was sober, I'd have just sent him to my house to catch the bat."

The door chimed and customers came in, a young woman and her mother. They were looking for silk flowers.

The morning passed quickly. It wasn't super busy in the shop, but it was steady. Nona went to the bakery for lunch while Rusty ate her apple and doughnut.

Rusty looked at the clock, it was 2:30, "Nona, can you lock up, I'm going to run out and check on Max, I need to see if his hand is still infected."

"Sure, go ahead," Nona answered.

"I promised I'd bring something for coffee, I'd better run to the bakery."

Rusty was out the front door and down the street before Nona could answer. Choosing a half dozen assorted rolls to bring to Max, she also chose one for Nona. When her stomach growled she realized the only things she had eaten all day was an apple and a jellied doughnut.

She asked, "Cindy, can you make me a cheese sandwich or something fast?"

"I sure can, I'll make you a special sandwich." A few minutes later Cindy came back with the sandwich in a bag. Rusty paid her and was out the door, sprinting down the sidewalk and into the shop.

"Here Nona, I brought you a treat for coffee. I'll see you in the morning."

Nona didn't answer; she turned 180 degrees and watched her boss rush through the shop and out the back door.

Rusty drove out of town and turned onto a gravel road. Taking her sandwich out of the bag with one hand, she shook it out of the wrapping. Savoring the first bite, she thought, Wow Cindy, you outdid yourself on a cheese sandwich. It had cheddar cheese, a tomato slice and onion. Then she had grilled it! I'll have to ask her what kind of bread spread she put on, it wasn't plain mustard, and it wasn't mayo. The sandwich was delicious.

The dust flew on the gravel road, she didn't think she was speeding, but her 25 minute drive took 20 minutes. This time she knew exactly where she was going.

It was a plus, driving up Max's driveway to the garage. She smiled to herself when she thought back to her tromp through the weeds and mud. The garage door was open and Max was in the garage working under the hood of a very old black car. Under the hood means the sides of the hood opened to reveal a very simple motor.

"Hi Max. Wow! Where did you get this relic?" Rusty asked coming around the back of the car.

"Hey," Max responded shutting and latching the hood. "This is more than just an old car. It belonged to my father. He bought it new in 1930, I've kept it running. I even take it out on the road once in a while."

Rusty walked around the car looking at the Greyhound dog hood ornament, the wooden spokes on the wheels; she noticed it said STOP on the brake lights.

"What kind of a car is this?" She wondered out loud.

Max answered, "This is a Whippet Classic; it was built in Toledo, Ohio, by Willy's. The first one came off the line in 1926. It replaced the Overlander."

Rusty had no clue what an Overlander was either, it didn't matter.

Max continued talking slowly, "My family didn't have much money and the Whippet was a cheaper vehicle so it was more affordable to poor farm families. They quit making them a year after Dad bought this one."

Rusty hadn't heard Max talk so much at one time. He was certainly proud of this old car.

"They built both the right handed and left handed models," he continued, "The right handed ones were shipped to Australia and New Zealand where they drive on the left side of the road."

Rusty opened the car door to look inside.

"So, what is this knob on the steering wheel, the horn?"

Reaching into the car to demonstrate, he answered, "Yes, but if you turn it clockwise the lights come on, first the parking lights, then the head lamps. You pull the knob to start the car, of course then you need to crank it, you do that from the front." Max went on, "All the wiring for this is at the bottom of the steering column under the carburetor. It isn't shielded from dripping gas so you'd have fires and lots of rewiring."

"Sounds dangerous to me," Rusty responded.

"It could be! Right handed cars didn't have that problem. When WW 2 started Willy's began building Jeeps, after the war they were made and sold to civilians."

"What did you bring for coffee today?" Max asked wiping his hands on an old greasy rag.

Rusty shut the door, "Do you like rolls? I have an assortment."

Max smiled and followed Rusty to her SUV to retrieve them.

"Do you know they call the Whippet the father of the SUV?" he said, eyeing her car.

Rusty laughed, "No I didn't, but I do now!" She handed Max the bag and followed him to the house.

Max said, "I'll put the coffee pot on, come on in."

He held the door for her, so she went into the kitchen. Once inside she was at a loss as to what to do. There wasn't anywhere to sit and she felt uncomfortable standing in the middle of the small room. Looking into the dining room she noticed the litter had been cleaned up and the magazines were gone. In fact the two rooms she could see looked neat and tidy.

"I'll wait on the porch." she said with a smile "it's such a beautiful afternoon. I love being outside."

Returning to the porch she took a seat on the top step. A couple fluffy white clouds floated in the bright blue sky. She watched as the sparrows darted in and out of a spruce tree. The black birds were back from where ever they go in the winter and were sitting on the tops of the apple trees on the west side of the house.

When Max returned, Rusty saw that he had taken the bandage off his hand to show her that he had been taking care of his cut. She took his hand and saw that the swelling was down. Even though it looked red and sore it was a lot better than it had been.

"This looks very good Max. But continue putting the antibiotic cream on it for a few days. If you keep it bandaged during the day, you could leave it uncovered at night to heal."

Max agreed and went inside to get the coffee while Rusty took a couple of rolls and napkins out of the bag.

"Do you drive the Whippet to town for groceries?" asked Rusty.

Max answered, "I don't have a license anymore; I guess they think I'm too old to drive, I turned 81 and couldn't pass the eye test. My neighbor takes me into Plains when I need to get groceries or go to the doctor. I just drive the Whippet around the section and stay on country roads. Not much traffic out here."

"Do you have children?"

"Two sons who live out of state, I don't see them, but they do call once in a while."

Rusty felt sad to hear that and decided she would just keep checking on him to make sure he stayed safe.

Max changed the subject, "I've been thinking the old chicken house sitting in the grove isn't in such bad shape, maybe I could get some chickens. It'd be sorta' nice to see some action out here. It gets a might lonely at times."

He looked at Rusty expectantly. She didn't know what to say! He certainly looked like he could care for a few chickens. Finally she said, "Max if you want chickens? You should have chickens."

Max grinned, "Ya! Then that's what I'll do! It'll take a little work getting the coop ready."

He got up and headed for the grove. Rusty stood up and quickly followed. They walked past the garage and the old out house. The door was standing open so she peeked inside. Two holes were covered with pieces of cardboard and a roll of toilet paper was tucked in an old coffee can, the end of the roll trailed over the edge, almost reaching the floor. She grimaced; no way could she use those facilities.

When she looked up Max was gone. She hurried in the direction he had went, through the brambles and bushes, and then spotted him going into a small building. When she caught up with him he was checking out nesting boxes nailed against the wall to the left of the door. She ducked to get in and stood hunched over looking around. To the right were four windows. Even though they went from the ceiling to the wooden floor they were only about three feet tall. They were unbroken, that was a plus, but they were so dirty, grimy, and buggy that they kept out the little light that could make it through the trees.

Max straightened up as much as he could and looked around, then commented, "It looks pretty solid."

Rusty thought, it looks like a big mess, but she didn't say so, dried leaves and assorted bugs clung to cobwebs that seemed to be hanging everywhere. She and Max were standing bent over looking at each other.

Max seemed energized. "Yep! Just needs a little cleaning."

Even though the ceiling was so low neither of them could stand straight, she supposed it would be fine. Chickens weren't very tall.

Rusty turned around and stepped over the threshold out into the fresh air and straightened up, stretching her back.

Max followed. He smiled. "Yes, I do believe I'll clean this up and get chickens. Let's go get another cup of coffee."

Rusty smiled too, Max seemed to have a new bounce to his step.

"I'll expect to see chickens when I come back again."

"Yes, Mum, you surely will,"

Rusty sat down on the top step while Max went into the house to refill their coffee cups. Returning he handed her a cup, then sat beside her and reached for another roll.

"I have a little problem Max and I'd like your input."

Rusty told him about coming home and finding the yellow roses on her counter. She told him about the note she found in the car that morning.

"I'm a little worried. I was perplexed about someone coming in my house when I wasn't home. I don't know if I should be scared or amused about the note I found."

Max was quiet for awhile. Then he said, "I'd say you have an admirer, but if he wants to make points he is going about it the wrong way. It could be innocent. Be careful and watchful, don't take chances. It might be a good idea to alert the police."

"I live in Sandy Bay and we have one policeman, Booga. I don't know how good it would be to tell him. It's a small town with not much going on, we don't need much protection. He'll issue a ticket once in a while; maybe pick someone up for drunkenness. Most of the drunks driving in town are his buddies, so if he picks anyone up it would be a tourist or someone from out of town."

"Well, just be careful and let me know if anything else happens, we'll think of some thing." Rusty was glad she had told Max about the flowers and note. He seemed genuinely concerned. She felt he was someone in whom she could confide.

It was a pleasant drive back to town. Too early for wild flowers, but she noted that the corn was peeking through the soil. The meadows were lush and green. Memorial Day was coming up, after that the summer heat and humidity would make the ditches explode with color.

Parking in the driveway, she heard talking and laughter coming from behind her house. Walking back she saw her neighbors had congregated around the fire pit. Jolly, chubby Glen waved and called, "come on out and play."

She waved back and nodded, then went into her house.

After freshening up, she chose a small bottle of Chardonnay out of the refrigerator, took a glass out of the cupboard, and then went to join them. Tonight the topic of discussion was embarrassing moments. Ava was telling of an incident that happened when they were young newlyweds. She was six months into her first pregnancy and living in Montana; Ava was scheduled to take a train back to Minnesota to visit her parents. They got into the car and drove around the block. Glen was going into the saloon on the corner to get his paycheck cashed so Ava would have some money for her trip. Ava waited in the car.

After Glen went into the saloon Ava decided she needed to use the restroom. So she went in after him. Thinking she should tell Glen she was using the facilities, she went up to where he was sitting at the bar, put her arm around his shoulder and whispered into his ear.

"Honey will you wait for me, I have to go to the bathroom." Glen turned his head and looked up at her and it wasn't Glen. It looked like Glen from the back; he had black hair, the clothes were the same, a yellow shirt and tan slacks. Ava ran to the restroom. She should have run out to the car. Because when she returned, Glen and this other man were standing by the door talking and laughing. Ava had to walk between them to leave the building; she could have died from embarrassment.

Ending the story, she said, "Poor guy, he looked up to see a big belly and a strange lady hitting on him." Everyone had a good laugh about that, even Ava.

By the time Rusty went into the house, it was dark, the sky clouded over and the wind had picked up. She heated up a can of tomato soup, took out the crackers and a couple cookies. "Boy," she thought, "My diet today is a disaster. I'll eat better tomorrow."

Settling into bed, she smiled thinking about Glen and Ava's embarrassing episode.

Chapter 7

M emorial Day arrived sunny with a brisk wind out of the north, the town bustled with activities. The VFW and American Legion members were getting ready to line up for the parade out to the cemetery. A memorial service to honor men and women who served in the armed forces is always held at the grave sites on a make shift stage. The names of the fallen military personal would be read, taps would be played to signify the closing of the day, followed by revelry to signal awaking to a new life.

Flags had been hung on the light posts, posters were put up for a bar-b-queue luncheon in the park; everyone seemed to be in high spirits. Even the tourists arriving from the campgrounds seemed to be caught up in the excitement.

Rusty took a jacket out of the back seat of her SUV and put it on just as Brad came around the side of her house.

Being he was single and such a nice guy the women in the park couldn't figure out why someone hadn't snagged him by now. It wasn't that he was ugly, on the contrary. Coaching sports at the high school kept him in good shape.

Maybe his sideburns were a little long. His sandy blonde hair made him look younger than he actually was, the ladies in the park all thought he was a handsome dude. Another plus was he could fix anything. She supposed that came with teaching Industrial Arts. If she wasn't so down on men she might consider him for herself.

"Are you heading for the parade Rusty?" he asked.

"I am," she answered, "I thought I'd get my exercise and walk."

"Let me give you a ride, you can walk home. I'm going to the BBQ at the park, and then driving to the cities for my niece's birthday party this afternoon. She is nine today."

"Sure, I'll take a ride," Rusty answered, "It feels chilly now, but it is supposed to warm up by this afternoon."

She followed Brad around to the back of her house, across the grassy area, to his red Toyota. Settling in the passenger's seat, Rusty asked, "Is the birthday girl your sister's daughter or your brother's daughter?"

"My sisters, I have no brother, it's just Jill and me." He chuckled, "She was such a tomboy she could have been a brother."

"Does this daughter take after her mother?"

"I think she does, probably more so than the other two girls." He continued, "When she was about seven she got stuck in a tree and couldn't get down. Her dad had to get a ladder and climb up to rescue her. The funny part is that there was an insurance agent at the house trying to sell them a health insurance policy. After that he looked like he wanted to change his mind."

Rusty giggled, then said, "Park behind my shop, we can walk to the parade and to the cemetery. After lunch you can easily leave for the cities without getting caught up in a traffic jam."

"Sounds good, I was hoping you'd say that," Brad answered with a smile. "That's why I asked you to ride along."

Rusty gave him a playful sock in the shoulder. He grinned at her and pulled up behind *Holly, Wood, and Wine.* He turned the car around so he'd be facing the street. Rusty opened the car door and got out; they walked together to Main Street. People had brought folding chairs and blankets to sit on, but blankets or chairs had slipped their minds so they sat down on the curb.

They heard the High School marching band and a few minutes later they saw two American Legion Soldiers leading the parade, carrying rifles over their shoulders. Flanked on each side of the men marched two Auxiliary women carrying flags. They were followed by the band, then more Legion members in uniform.

The Veterans of Foreign Wars came next, with some riding in convertibles. Behind them were the Girl Scouts and Boy Scouts. When they had passed by, the people who planned on walking to the cemetery got in line to follow the parade. Rusty and Brad joined them, while others went to get their cars.

The ceremony at the cemetery was brief. With no trees or buildings to block the wind it was chilly. People who ventured to the service hugged themselves trying to keep warm. Those who had blankets wrapped them around their children. The Pastor stepped upon the small stage and took a microphone. After giving a short message, he read the names of the servicemen and the wars in which they fought. During the 21 gun salute, the townspeople stood with quiet respect, but when it was over they rushed to their cars.

Brad and Rusty saw Carol and Jessie heading for their car. Carols husbands name had been read; he lost his life in Viet Nam.

"Are you going to the BBQ?" Brad called.

"Yes," answered Carol, "Hop in; it seems like the wind is picking up, I'll give you a ride."

Traffic was heavy, so they poked along, driving and stopping.

"When we get to the park, just drop me off and I'll get the food vouchers while you find a place to park" said Brad. "You girls save me a place in line, it will go quicker and I'm starved."

Rusty reached for her purse, but Brad stopped her. "My treat, I'm buying lunch." Then he added, "Tickets are only $8 and I appreciate the ride and company."

"Thank you kind sir that is very nice, I'll bake you some cookies," offered Carol.

"I don't bake," Jessie said, "but thanks."

Rusty laughingly added, "And I let you park in my lot."

Letting her passengers out of the car, Carol went to find a parking space. Brad stopped at the table to buy food vouchers for everyone while Rusty and Jessie saved places for them in the food line.

"It seems much warmer here," said Jessie.

"Yes." answered Rusty, "The trees and bushes act as a windbreak. Smelling the heavenly fragrance of pulled pork seems to make me forget the chill."

"Don't forget they have beans and potato salad. Look at the different types of bars, how can you pick just one?" Jessie asked.

Brad and Carol arrived just as they were about to pick up their Styrofoam plates.

"Ahhh! Comfort food, this is perfect timing." Brad commented with a laugh as he handed the ladies their vouchers.

Finding four empty seats together at the picnic was a challenge. But then they spotted Fred and Marsha sitting alone near the playground. They headed that way. Fred spotted them and waved them over to share the table. It was a little wild with their two boys racing around the merry-go-round.

Marsha was a good customer, she loved to shop. She was in and out of Rusty's shop often, checking for new merchandise. Fred had been elected to the city council last fall.

Carol and Jess ate quickly, picking up their empty plates they went off to chat with friends.

Brad excused himself and asked, "can I give you a ride home Rusty? I should be going so I'm not late for the party."

"Thank you, no, I'm going to stay and visit awhile." She answered.

When they were alone, Marsha asked, "Have you heard anything about a Federal Agent from the Drug Task force who is said to be scouting around town?"

"Gosh no," said Rusty, "why would a small town like Sandy Bay need someone from the drug task force here?"

Marsha answered, "Rumor has it that a business here in town is a drop for drugs."

"That is just a rumor Marsha," chided Frank. "They don't know for sure. No one seems to know anything positive. Not even the council has heard anything official."

"I haven't even heard the rumor." Rusty stated, "I can't imagine which business would agree to doing something that harmful." She hated rumors, didn't listen to them and wouldn't repeat them.

"I really should run I'd like to stop at the shop and see if everything is in order before I open for business tomorrow."

Holly, Wood, and Wine was a quiet retreat from the traffic outside. Residents were going home and visitors were leaving town. Rusty made notes of products on which she was running low. Tomorrow she would call for more wood products. The smaller shelves were selling as well as the bird houses and smaller treasure chests. The young teen girls that came in were after earrings and bracelets. Organic bath bombs and soaps was a bit of an attraction as well with the older teen girls and young adults. Rusty was happy the artists that supplied her with their crafts were doing such a good business.

She rearranged some shelves, adding to them from items in the stockroom. When she left the shop at 4:30 she was wishing she had driven her car. She was a power walker and could do a fifteen minute mile, but all at once she felt tired.

"Oh well," she said out loud, "It's a nice afternoon now that the wind went down and I'll have time to think."

As she walked a black car came up behind her, slowed down and passed. A few minutes later the same car had turned around and cruised by again. Feeling a little paranoid she put the strap of her shoulder bag around her neck, tucked it under her arm, broke into a run and trotted the last couple blocks to the park road. She didn't notice the black car driving by again as she fumbled for her keys to unlock the door.

Rusty poured a glass of lemonade, then took the furniture polish, a rag, and began dusting upstairs in her bedroom. She was finished in record time and her tiny house smelled like lemon. After vacuuming and washing her bathroom and kitchen floors, she added an ice cube to her half empty glass and sat down on the love seat waiting for the floor to dry. She closed her eyes and dozed.

The train whistle blew as it crossed over the highway on its way out of town. Rusty sat up and was surprised to see it was getting dark. She stretched, got up and walked out onto her deck. No one was around. All was quiet. She went back inside and made an egg salad sandwich, grabbed a bag of chips, a bottle of water and headed for the lake. It was a pleasant night. Sitting with her back to a big Maple tree, she slipped off her shoes and wiggled her toes. In the moonlight she watched a pair of loons swim by with a baby on mama's back. The birds had called it a night; the whole world seemed to have settled down. It felt peaceful.

Rusty's thoughts went back to her conversation with Marsha and Fred. If there was anything to the rumor of a task force in town, which business owner would be so thick headed as to encourage a drug trade in a small tourist town such as Sandy Bay. She couldn't think of one.

After putting the crust of her sandwich into the empty Doritos bag and crumpling it, she tucked it into her shoe. Standing up she took off her tee shirt and slipped out of her jeans, then walked into the lake in her underwear. When it reached her knees she dove in, letting the frigid water wash over her body. She felt alive, refreshed and cold. After turning on her back and doing couple of back strokes, she stood up and hurried back to shore. Shivering she put on her clothes and ran home.

Chapter 8

Memorial Day was on Monday; Tuesday morning when Rusty opened her refrigerator it didn't reveal much food. The bread, gone! The milk, gone! No eggs! No jelly! She checked the coffee canister, not much!

She decided to go to the bakery for breakfast. It was a beautiful sunny morning. She locked her house and took off on foot. Entering the bakery she was hit with the aroma of fresh baked bread, bacon, eggs and coffee. Her stomach rumbled with delight. Looking around she figured a lot of people must have had empty refrigerators, the five tables and 3 booths were occupied. Rusty slid onto a stool at the counter.

"Hi Cindy," she greeted the waitress. "I'll have one egg and toast, and a gallon of coffee."

Cindy already had a mug in one hand and a coffee pot in the other.

"I saw you coming." She said with a smile, "I'm ready for you; I know what you're like without your morning cup of Joe. Your food will be right up."

Rusty smiled and picked up the cup, "Thank you, you're a life saver."

While she sipped her coffee, she reached for the menu and began reading the back, *"The History of Sandy Bay."* It didn't surprise her to learn it began as a railroad town. That's how a lot of Minnesota towns got their beginning. She tried to picture what it must have looked like in the middle 1800's. She'd seen pictures of hitching rails in front of small buildings, with big windows. The dirt or muddy streets and wooden sidewalks must have been a real mess. She didn't think it would make much difference if the dust was flying or the water was sloshing down the streets.

Cindy set her plate down before her and refilled her coffee.

"Thanks Cindy, I'm starving," Rusty commented returning the menu to its original place behind the napkin holder.

The door opened, a big man wearing a blue shirt and pants entered and stood inside looking around. He came over and sat down by Rusty leaving an empty stool between them.

"Good morning," he greeted her; he removed his baseball cap and placed it in his lap. Rubbing his bald head he reached over and picked up the menu.

Rusty smiled and returned the greeting. When you sit at the counter you eat with whoever sits down by you.

Cindy brought him a mug and the coffee pot. He ordered a grand slam.

Rusty guessed that was a ton of food, but decided he could definitely hold it all. She picked up her toast and dipped it in the egg yolk.

The man never said another word until he had finished eating.

Rusty laid some money on the counter and rose to leave.

He got up too, putting down a ten dollar bill.

"You don't know me," he said, "but I know who you are."

His eyes skimmed the room. "I'd like to talk to you. This isn't the place. I'll get a message to you later. In the mean time be watchful."

Rusty watched him stride toward the door, pulling his cap down securely on his head, and disappearing down the street.

Booga, who had been sitting in the corner booth, quickly followed him out the door.

"Be watchful? Be watchful of what?"

Rusty sat back down at the counter. "Cindy, can I have a coffee to go?" Taking a couple more dollars out of her purse she laid them on the counter.

When Cindy returned with the coffee, Rusty asked in a low voice. "Do you know who that man was?"

"I don't," she answered, "he has been coming in off and on for a couple of weeks, I think he must be working around here. I don't know where."

"Strange," Rusty whispered, "He told me to be watchful."

Cindy shrugged. "I don't know what that is about."

Rusty walked down the block to her shop. She had given Nona the day off as she had guessed they wouldn't be busy the day after a three day week end. The campers had packed up and left. The town seemed quiet except for the locals and many of them were returning to their day jobs.

Down time is rare and Rusty had done what needed to be done yesterday. The worst thing to do is have free time and not have any idea of what to do. She took a pad and began writing down ideas for new products to sell in the shop. Then she organized her desk. The morning drug on, so she tore apart one corner of store and rearranged everything, giving it a new look.

It was two o'clock and she'd waited on three customers.

A middle aged man had bought a bird house. A local housewife picked up 2 bottles of wine, they chatted for twenty minutes or so, discussing (not gossiping) about changes taking place in town. The third customer was a browser, killing time waiting while her husband got a hair cut.

Rusty locked the shop up early and began to walk home to get her car. She needed to go to the grocery store. Being out of everything she knew it was too much to carry.

She was almost home when she heard sirens. The ambulance screamed by with Booga hot on its tail. She supposed it must be an accident and hoped it wasn't too serious. They turned left on the road past the tiny houses and went out into the country. Rusty crossed the street to Lakeside Park and unlocked her door.

When she returned from the grocery store she noticed Ernie and Glen arranging wood in the fire pit and strolled back to see what was happening.

"Bon fire tonight?" she asked.

"We're roasting Brats," replied Glen, "You're expected to be here at six, and not one minute past."

"Okay, I just come from the store so I'll bring fixings for S'mores."

"Bring lots, and I'll have S'more, S'more, S'more." Ernie laughed at his own joke.

Rusty just raised one eye brow, and grinned.

That evening when Rusty carried the goodies out to the pergola she saw the guys had the fire going. Ava and Rose were setting out the buns and brats, covering them to keep the bugs out. There didn't seem to be any bugs, but just in case one showed up for the picnic. Brad came with plates and plastic utensils. Bruce came walking from his house by the lake with two large bags of chips and a bowl of his homemade salsa. The table was filling up with food.

Ernie said, "Hey Brad, what do a call a cowboy who helps out at school?"

"Are you guys picking on me 'cuz I work at school? I have no clue."

"A deputy head," Ernie replied with a laugh.

"That makes no sense." Brad snorted.

"Is this cowboy joke night?" Bruce stated, "Why did the cowboy get a hot seat?"

"Why?" Glen responded.

"Because he rode the range!"

Rusty giggled, but Brad just commented, "Ouch! That's a sick joke."

Trina came carrying a bowl of cut up fruit. "Did anyone hear where the ambulance went?"

There were murmurs of "No," "Not me." "Uhah." "I haven't."

Setting her bowl on the table, she said, "I was just at the grocery store and I heard some man hung himself in the woods behind the campground."

"Really?" Jessie questioned, "That's terrible. Who was it?

"I didn't hear who it was; I don't suppose anyone can release names until the family is notified."

"Who found the body? Did you hear?"

"They were saying it was a campground volunteer, he was picking up litter and cleaning restrooms after the week end. Actually his dog was going nuts. He walked back into the woods to see why he was so riled up, and found this man hanging in a tree."

Anne sympathized with the volunteer, "That had to be so traumatic, I'd have nightmares for months if I came across something like that."

"Good thing the dog found him," Rusty added.

Jessie and Carol began taking ketchup, mustard, and pickle relish out of a paper bag and setting them on the table next to the buns.

Glen handed out sticks and long handled forks.

It wasn't until Friday when the Weekly Gazette arrived from Plaines that they discovered the name of the suicide victim. Thomas Miller, he was a federal officer who was on an assignment in the area.

When Rusty read that, the thought crossed her mind that maybe the Drug Task story was real.

The newspaper had taken the picture off his driver's license and printed that in the paper along with the write-up. The article stated it was being treated as a homicide.

Rusty looked at the picture and gasped. It was the man who warned her to be watchful.

Chapter 9

The summer heat, humidity and tourists all arrived in Sandy Bay about the same time. Rusty and Nona were kept busy along with the artists that supplied their store. Rusty was taking care of a customer at the till and Nona was unpacking a box of aprons in the back room when the door bell chimed.

Rusty looked up, a young man wearing a Twins baseball cap smiled at her and began browsing throughout the shop. Once in a while he would stop to examine a wood item or a clay pot then set it down. He smiled again at Rusty when she joined him and held out his hand.

"Good morning, my name is Kevin Barker, if you're not busy, I'd like to talk to you."

Rusty shook his hand, "My name is Hope Albert, but everyone calls me Rusty. Talk away, or would you like somewhere more private?"

Kevin removed his cap and Rusty noticed his carrot red hair and freckles. He seemed a little self conscience but continued; "I'm looking for a job and was wondering if you could use extra help for the summer?"

"Let's go to the office, I'll get us some coffee. Do you drink coffee? Would you prefer something else?"

"Coffee's fine," he answered.

"Nona, will you watch the front? I'll be in my office if you need anything"

Nona was hanging the aprons on hangers, "Sure, no problem. I'll go out front when I hear the door chime."

Rusty directed Kevin to a seat, handed him a cup, then sat behind her desk. "What kind of work are you looking for?" She asked.

"Whatever you have for me, I'm a junior in college over at Plains, taking a business management and marketing course. I'd like to work for you to get some experience in the retail field. Someday I'd like to open my own shop. I'm pretty sure I'd like to pursue this as a career.

"What kind of a shop would you be interested in opening?"

"I'm thinking of a sporting goods store in a vacation community like this, selling hunting and fishing equipment. I need a summer job and if I can work at your shop I'll know if it's a really something I want to do."

Rusty looked at him thoughtfully. "We could use some help around here," she said, "I wouldn't be able to pay much; everything we sell is on consignment."

Kevin smiled, "It's not the money," he said, "It's the experience."

Rusty stood up, offered him her hand, "You've got yourself a summer job. I can offer you minimum wage if it is acceptable to you."

Kevin took her hand, "It's a deal, when can I start?"

"How about starting Monday morning? That will give me the week end to map out a job plan."

"Sounds good, I'll see you Monday morning." He rose and started for the door then turned. "Is nine o'clock okay?"

"Perfect," Rusty answered, they walked together to the front of the store. Two young women were just leaving.

"Nona, meet Kevin Barker, our new employee."

Nona welcomed Kevin and when he put on his cap and left she looked at Rusty, "I didn't know we were hiring."

"I didn't either, but when he asked for a job, I thought about the dirty windows, unpacked boxes in the back, the storage room really needs cleaning and organizing. He wants to own a sporting goods store one day. A good way to start is at the bottom."

"Nona did that woman look familiar to you?" Rusty asked.

"You mean one that just left? I don't think I've seen either of them before. She isn't a local if that's what you mean. She did buy one of the smaller chests. I'll admit they are beautiful."

"That's great. I know Mr. Wilson can use the extra money, even though he doesn't make much on each item," Rusty answered.

"I must be imagining things," she looked perplexed, "but there is something about her, maybe she has been in the shop before."

The door chimed and one very angry woman came in, complaining to her friend. "That jerk face ate my plant. That is why I can't have nice things. It struggled for years! Just when it started to grow and flourish; that's when some big butt head ate it to the dirt. THEN he had the nerve to stick his face in the pot and look at me like — MA - where's my snack? I just told him "Sir, you are on the naughty list this year."

Her friend holding back her laughter, mouth the words "HER CAT" at Rusty and Nona who stood there staring at the ladies.

Nona whispered to Rusty, "let's set those plants out that we transplanted and brought into the shop yesterday."

Rusty nodded, and went to the front to clear off a shelf in front of the window. Nona brought out three plants freshly potted into homemade clay pots. The cat lady ended up buying a spider plant to replace the plant her cat ate.

Her friend teased her, "You'll be hanging that one from the ceiling out of the reach of Butt Face the jerk."

Nona left at five and Rusty shortly after. It was a beautiful walk home. Everything looked so fresh and green. She heard a lawn mower in the distance, a couple of teenage girls rode past on their bikes. The smell of grilled meat coming from a back porch reminded her that it had been hours since she had eaten. Her stomach growled.

Rusty unlocked her back door and turned when Jessie called to her. "We're meeting under the pergola in 20 minutes."

She waved to Jessie and stepped into the house anxious to get out of her shoes and into her flip flops.

Twenty minutes later she walked out back with her drink and a small bag of Doritos. She saw that Jacob was wearing shorts and Ann was giving him a bad time about rushing the season.

Ann was saying, "It isn't that hot that you have to show off your hairy legs."

Jacob answered, "You think I should shave them? Yes, it certainly is hot and humid! It's just that you spend most of the year down south and are acclimatized."

Ann argued "You haven't thawed out yet from the Minnesota winter."

Jacob's wife Peg asked, "Why does 65 degree feel warmer in the spring than 65 degree's does in the fall?"

Bruce piped up, "Being we're talking about temperature, do you know you can tell the temperature by counting how many times a cricket chirps on a hot summer night?"

"Oh you can not," argued Ann, "your just saying that."

"Nope, not just saying, it is a fact that a cricket chirps in 13 second intervals. Take that number and add 40. So if a cricket chirps 25 times in 13 seconds add 40 and it is about 65 degrees out."

"Or you could just buy a thermometer smarty," said Ann under her breath.

Bruce laughed, "I didn't get this old without learning a few things on the way."

Rusty changed the subject and shared, "I hired a new employee that will be starting work on Monday. He seems like a nice young man. You'll all have to come in and welcome him to Sandy Bay."

Ava answered, "I will drop in, and I've been meaning to ask if you have room in the shop for some of my items I made in Arizona last winter?"

Rusty's stomach growled again, this time so loud everyone heard it and laughed. She grinned and said, "I guess the Doritos's didn't do it." Then she added, "I do have room Ava, but I'll probably not put any knit items out till later this summer."

She rose and laughingly stated, "I'd better get something to eat, or they'll hear my stomach all the way into town."

When Rusty returned to her house she saw that her door was open. That's odd she thought I'm sure I closed it. She carefully pushed it wider and peered in, she didn't see anyone, and maybe she did leave it ajar. Stepping into the small kitchen she noticed something on the counter. Looking closer she saw it was a box of assorted chocolates.

"What the heck! Not again!" She said out loud. Looking around, she saw nothing else was out of order.

Still mumbling under her breath, "I know it's not anyone from the park we were all together out back. Who ever put it there must have parked on the road walked to her house. Who is doing this?"

Rusty sank down on her floral loveseat, her mind whirling. Then she got up and locked the door. There are thirteen people living in the park, all thirteen were at out back in the yard. But did anyone come later? She tried to think. It couldn't be Jacob or Ann, they were arguing when she got there. Bruce was tending the fire pit, and Brad left his house the same time as I did, we arrived together. It couldn't be roly, poly Ernie, him and Rose did come later, but from the lake; they had been fishing with Glen and Ava on the pontoon. The four of them came carrying their beer, crackers and dip. Jessie and Carol were washing the bird poop off the picnic table. Only Trina came later. Being she worked as a bookkeeper for Jacob's construction company she usually got home about 5:30 unless she runs errands then it's later. "I'm positive Trina wouldn't be leaving the notes and gifts. Would she? No! She's way too busy." Rusty shook her head; she'd have to tell Booga, this was scaring her.

When her stomach rumbled again she got up and put some water in a pan on the stove. She added a cup of noodles when the water began to boil and measured out ¼ cup of sour cream. To save dishes, she piled a tablespoon of butter on top of the measuring cup of sour cream. A tablespoon of grated parmesan cheese balanced on that, along with ¼ teaspoon of Italian seasoning and 1/8th teaspoon garlic powder. After draining the noodles she carefully dumped it all together and stirred. After adding a dash of pepper, she emptied the pan onto a paper plate, sprinkled a handful of shredded parmesan cheese on top, poured another glass of wine and returned to sit on the loveseat.

She needed to think about something else, so she picked up the remote, turned on the television, putting her feet up on the small coffee table she began watching NCIS.

Before going up to bed, Rusty found a pair of gloves in her winter coat pocket and carefully put the box of candy in a plastic grocery bag. If the police could get some useful prints off the box, maybe they'd be able to identify the person leaving her gifts.

Chapter 10

Running, running, running she's in the woods. Branches catching at her clothes, she's slipping on wet leaves; her heart is banging in her chest. She stops to listen. And then takes off again, coming out of the trees into a cornfield. She stops a few rows in and crouches. "Brrrrrrrrring!" Rusty sat up! She is wet with sweat! Her blanket is knotted in a ball and her pillow is on the floor. She reached over and turned off the alarm. It's only a dream. No a nightmare! Lying back she tried to remember who was chasing her? Where was she? Was it a premonition? Was it a sense of coming events? She shuttered, got up, and padded downstairs to the bathroom.

Thirty minutes later, she picked up the candy box safely secured in a plastic bag, put on the alarm, locked her door and drove to the store. Instead of going in she walked to the bakery hoping to find Booga eating his breakfast. He was sitting in a corner booth with his back to the wall. With him was a man in a cowboy hat. She hadn't seen him around before. He looked about 50ish; his dark sideburns peeking out of his hat had a tinge of gray. It didn't look like a razor had brushed his face this morning. His stubble could have been more than a day old.

Rusty hesitated, unsure if she should approach them. Walking up to the counter she ordered a cup of coffee and toast and then carried it to a table where she could watch to see when the stranger left and Booga would be alone. Of course that didn't happen. The stranger slid out of the booth and Booga stood up, put some money on the table and left with him. Rusty sat there and finished her toast before following them out the door.

The men were down the block near her shop, standing beside an older blue Ford pick-up deep in conversation. The stranger towered over Booga, his hat and high healed boots added to his height. Booga watched as he got into his truck and drove away. Then he began walking toward Rusty.

She stopped him and asked, "I need to talk to you Booga, would you have time to come to my shop?"

Booga looked surprised, agreed, and walked with Rusty down the block.

"What's up?" he asked, as Rusty unlocked the door and took off the alarm.

Neither Nona nor Kevin had arrived for work. They were alone.

Rusty set the bag on the counter and replied, "I'm being stalked."

Booga listened carefully while she recounted the incident with the roses, the note, thinking she was followed, and now the candy.

"You're sure it's no one in the park?" Booga asked.

"No." Rusty picked up the bag and handed it to him. "I didn't touch it; I was hoping you could find finger prints on the box."

Taking the bag, He responded, "That only works if the prints are in the system, I'll see what I can do."

Booga looked around the shop, barely glancing at the corner that held the aprons, dish towels and other fancy work. He noted the wine, clay pots and pottery. His eyes fell on the wood work, the chests, bird houses, and shelves; he seemed to be studying the items. He started to say something when Kevin and Nona came in the back door. They were talking and laughing. They stopped when they saw the town cop.

Booga looked back at the woodwork, glancing at the stained glass items he said, "I'll let you know what I find out." Then he left without so much as a hello, how are you, not even a nod of his head toward her employees.

"What's up with him?" Nona asked, "He looks like he has a burr up his butt."

Kevin went "PSSST" and laughed, spitting his gum across the room. Still laughing he retrieved it and walked behind the counter to the waste basket.

"I'm sorry, but that was funny."

Nona was laughing too, "Not as funny as your gum shooting across the room."

Rusty grinned, happy to see that they got along so well despite the age difference. Nona seemed to mother Kevin and he seemed to enjoy being mothered. He had only been working a couple of weeks and had caught on quickly.

Since he came the supply room was organized, the shelves were clean, stocked and the windows shone. He even had some good ideas on decorating. His charm and marketing skills made him a good salesman.

It was the middle of June; the tourist season was in full swing. In the campground recreational vehicles and tents sprawled along the lake. The men fished and the women shopped. Business was good and that made up for the slower winter months.

"Before anyone comes in I want to have a short meeting." Rusty stated. "Then I'm going into my office to do some bookwork, and the shop is yours."

"What's up? You look so serious." Nona commented.

Kevin added, "And a little sad, does it have to do with Booga being here?"

"Yes," Rusty bit her bottom lip. "I'll answer all your questions, but let me start at the beginning." Nona knows about the yellow roses I found on my kitchen cupboard. I also found a note in my car. And now it's a box of chocolates that arrived mysteriously while I was out back with the neighbors, practically just behind my house. Walking home one night I felt I was being followed by a black car. That could be my imagination, but truthfully I don't feel safe in my own home."

Looking at Kevin she added, "Yes, that is why Booga was here."

Kevin pondered that, and then answered, "Do you know what you need? A dog!"

"That's an idea Kevin," Nona responded, "No one will be hanging around your house without you knowing."

"I don't think so; there is no room in my house for a dog."

"I have a dog, he's trained, and I'll let him stay with you, just try it and see what happens. You can bring him to the shop during the day, or he'll be just as happy hanging out in your house."

"Thanks, but no thanks." Rusty turned to go to her office, "I've got bookwork to do, call me if you need anything."

Rusty went to the back room to start the coffee pot. Before it was done dripping she poured herself a cup then went into the office. She was glad she decided to hire another employee; she didn't need to come in Sundays to catch up on the paperwork.

"I'm going to lunch; can I bring you back a sandwich?"

Rusty looked up surprised, "Is it that time already? Where did the morning go?"

"Kevin is back and its 1 o'clock."

She took some money out of the desk drawer and handed it to Nona. "Sure a tuna sandwich is good; bring back a dozen assorted cookies. You and Kevin can have some for afternoon coffee and I'll take the rest out to Max."

Then she continued, "I need a couple more pictures for next year's calendar, so I'll go out, check on Max and bring my camera. I was going to wait for the fall colors, but I should get the pictures to the printer. The afternoon sun might give a different effect."

Nona turned, "Sure, I'll be back in a bit."

It was close to three o'clock when Rusty finally left the shop and pointed her SUV east. Turning off the highway onto a gravel road that angled a little northeast, she drove slowly to keep the dust down; it was a beautiful summer afternoon. The cumulus clouds floated across the blue sky. The ditches along the country road were lined with yellow dandelions, prairie milkweed and wild yarrow. The grasshoppers were out all ready. Using their back legs to catapult them into the air they took flight knocking the seeds off the puffy dandelions.

Pulling up into Max's driveway, she took the cookies, and out of habit, locked her purse in the car. Putting her keys in her pocket, she walked toward the house. Max was down by the barn pumping a pail of water. He looked up when he heard the car. Rusty waved and set the white bag of cookies on porch floor. Max waved back and continued pumping. Rusty walked down to join him.

"Hey there, I need a couple more pictures of old buildings for my calendar, want to go for a ride with me to see what we find?" Trying to convince him she wheedled, "It is a pretty day for a ride!"

Max's eyes lit up. His pink tongue darted out licking his lips. Then he smiled through his white stubble. "I think that would be great, there is a couple things I should do first, are you in a hurry?"

"No, just so the sun doesn't get away from us, it's no hurry."
"Hey, you shaved!"

"Sure I always shave in the summer, it is cooler, and by fall it has grown back for winter."

Max lifted the pail off the spout and set it down on the hard packed dirt. Then he kneeled and removed a wooden cover from the top of the well.

Rusty peered down the deep dark hole. Max reached in and grabbed a rope that was attached to the rusty pump underneath the board and began to pull; a long slender bucket with a cover on it came into view. The rope was attached to the handle.

"I've never seen a pail like that before."

Max pulled it out and set it on the ground. "It's an old cream can, it belonged to my folks," he answered taking off the cover. Max reached in and took out some white wrapped packages. Then reached into the bottom and pulled out a pound of butter. He handed that to Rusty. Sorting through the white packages he chose one and handed that one to her too. "That is dried beef," He stated. Replacing the rest of the packages he put the cover back on the can and lowered it into the well. Checking to make sure the rope was still secure, he replaced the wood cover and with some effort stood up. He looked down at Rusty still sitting on the ground, holding the butter and beef, he continued, "And that my friend is my refrigerator." Max chuckled, "If you don't shut your mouth it will be full of flies."

Rusty snapped her mouth shut and stared at Max.

"Come let's go to the house, you carry that, I'll take the water."

Neither said a word until they reached the kitchen. Max set the pail by the sink, and turned to take the butter and beef from Rusty.

That is when Rusty exclaimed, "What century are you living in?"

Max laughed, and walked into the pantry. "I do have a Styrofoam cooler. Things stay pretty good in there for awhile. Butter doesn't need to be refrigerated, it gets hard. Dried beef is cured, that is good and I'll eat it up in a couple of days. I'll have creamed chipped beef over potatoes tonight and a sandwich tomorrow."

"You're sure proving to me that people can live without all the conveniences we call the necessities of life"

Max laughed, "I've been thinking, my friend Fred died a couple years or so ago, no one has lived on his farm since. Maybe his barn or one of his sheds would be okay for your calendar." Then he continued, "Yes, I think Fred would like that. In fact he'd get a kick out of it seeing his old buildings in print."

Rusty chided, "Now your being a crazy old man if you think Fred would even know his buildings were on a calendar page."

"You never know, stranger things have happened."

"Let's go look, we'll see."

The sun was moving across the sky, sometimes the bright afternoon sun didn't work for the look she wanted to capture. She just hoped it wasn't too dark when they got to the farm.

Rusty backed her car out slowly to the end of the driveway. "Which way?" She asked, and then followed the directions to turn right out onto the gravel road. A squirrel decided to dart across the road just as she rolled ahead. Slamming on the brakes, both she and Max pitched forward.

"Better put your seat belt on when you ride with me." Rusty stated. "I duck for flying birds too!"

"The pinecones are always better on the other side of the road," quipped Max fastening his seat belt, "that squirrel will meet his waterloo one day. I hope it isn't me who takes him to his destiny."

Rusty sped up to the speed limit, what ever that was on a dusty country road. "Tell me about your friend Fred."

"Well," Max thought awhile, "We've been friends since country school. Took the bus together to high school in Plains, then we farmed about 5 miles apart from each other. He was like a brother."

Rusty followed directions to a driveway that looked in better shape than it should after being abandoned for a couple years (or so). She pulled up under a huge cottonwood tree and shut off the motor.

"You walk around and snap your pictures; I'll poke around here and reminisce about the good old days. Take your time!"

Rusty stepped high through the grass, knowing when she got home she'd be checking for wood ticks. She hated those blood sucking insects worse than mosquitoes or flies.

She saw the old barn, some boards near the top was hanging loose, the hip roof caved in like a sway back old nag. This might work she thought to herself. The sky was beginning to turn a rosy hue; maybe she didn't need the fall colors. Kneeling to position the barn in the right light she clicked away. Making her way to the back of the barn, she saw what looked like a straw building. Ever curious, she walked to the front and peered into the dim interior. It looked like an old chicken house. Nests were nailed to the back wall in a double row. The door was hanging loose and torn plastic hung from openings that were most likely windows. After taking some pictures at various angles, she gingerly pushed the door. Stepping inside she saw rusty old feeders, and watering cans strewn about. In the dim light she noticed a pile of wooden objects thrown under the nests in the corner. A closer look and she saw birdhouses and chests like she sold in her shop. The roofs were torn off the birdhouses and the inside linings were torn loose on the chests. Picking one up she turned it over. A label with the name of her store and the price tag was still stuck to the bottom. Jack Wilson (the artist) was wood burned into a corner. It was her merchandise. She picked up one bird house and one chest and turned to leave. That is when she heard a rustling and "Ummmmm!" coming from the dark corner behind the door. Stopping dead in her tracks, she listened; it came again, rustling and "Ummmmmm". Curiously and with caution she moved toward the door. Moving it slowly she peered into the dark corner. Her heart leaped into her throat and she felt real fear when the outline of a body came into view.

"Ummmmm!" whoever it was begin trashing around and the sounds became more desperate. When Rusty's eyes adjusted to the dim light, she saw it was a woman, bound and gagged. She could just make out silver duck tape over her mouth. Laying the bird house and chest on the ground she knelt by her side. Grabbing a corner of the duck tape and prying it loose, she gave a quick pull. The woman grimaced with pain, tears glistened in her eyes.

"What on earth happened to you? Are you hurt? Can you walk?"

"Quick, get that duck tape off my feet and let's get out of here before they come back."

She heard pleading and panic in the woman's voice. Rusty worked as fast as her shaky hands would allow. Finding the end of the tape and prying it loose, then unwrapping about two feet of tape seemed to take forever. She helped the unsteady woman to her feet and steadied her when she swayed.

"Let's go!" the woman whispered as she stumbled toward the door.

Rusty picked up the bird house and chest and followed her. She began to run wobbly toward the woods.

"No," Rusty called, "the car is this way."

The woman turned and followed Rusty through the weeds to the driveway.

She felt relieved when she saw her car was still where she parked. It was dumb of her not to take the keys with her. Opening the back door, she threw the broken items on the floor and helped the woman into the car.

Where was Max? Rusty called and waited, then called again.

He came slowly walking out of the woods.

"Are you done already?" Max answered.

"Hurry, Max, we have to get out of here, NOW!"

Max looked surprise, and tried to hurry, but his hurry was still too slow for Rusty. She got in the drivers seat, buckled up and waited impatiently for Max to open the door. He put his left leg in then grabbed the bar above the door and hoisted himself up onto the seat. She was backing out of the yard the second the door slammed.

"Buckle up Max." she almost yelled at him.

He was so surprised, he obeyed instantly.

They were down the road and around the corner before Max dared ask. "What the world happened? Where is the fire?"

Rusty didn't answer; she was busy keeping the speeding car on the narrow road. She was hoping she didn't meet anyone as she doubted there was enough room to pass. When she turned onto a larger county road, she looked at Max.

"Look into the back seat if you can, we have a passenger."

Max turn to look, the woman was lying down, crying softly, tears were streaming down her face, she couldn't even them wipe away because her hands were still bound.

Max quietly stared out the front window while Rusty told him the story of how she found the woman bound and gagged behind the door of the chicken house. She didn't mention finding her merchandise.

Everything was quiet from the back seat.

"When last were you at your friend Fred's?"

"Not since he passed away. I had no reason to go out there. It was nice walking around through the woods where we played as kids. We hunted there as teens. The woods go back quite away; there are choke cherry trees in the back."

"Did you go into the house?"

"No, why on earth would I do that?"

Rusty turned into Max's driveway and parked in front of the garage. Shutting the car off she put her arm on the back of the seat, un-clicking her seat belt with her left hand. She turned to face him. Glancing in the back, she saw the woman was lying still. Her eyes were closed. She whispered, "Let's talk outside."

"Max, in my shop I sell items made by artists in the community. The bird houses and chests are a good seller. I found a bunch of my merchandise in a corner of the old chicken house behind the barn. The roofs were off the birdhouses and the covers on the chests have had the inside linings torn apart. I heard gossip that drugs were being sold and a business place in town is the drug drop. Max, what if it is my shop?"

"Who makes the wood items?" He asked.

"An older retired man, Jack Wilson; I can't believe he is involved in drugs."

"I don't know him, but you could be right. Maybe someone is planting the drugs after the items are made and before it gets to your shop."

"I have to go Max; I need to go to the police."

"I think you should come in, we need to talk about this and not go off half cocked."

"Maybe your right,"

Rusty opened the car door and looked in the back, really noticing the woman for the first time. She knew her, in spite of her tousled hair full of straw, the bruised cheek and black eye, it was the woman who had come into her shop to buy a chest and left without her change.

"Let's go in and talk," she said, helping the woman sit up. Holding her arm Rusty steadied her as they walked to the house.

Max led the way, stopping to pick up the white bag of cookies setting on the porch before walking up the stairs and into the house.

"Gosh, it's after 7:00 already, where has the time gone?" stated Max.

While Rusty worked the duck tape off the woman's hands, Max took the tea kettle and filled it with water. After setting it down on the cook stove he lifted the lid, arranged some corn cobs and kindling in the belly, and then lit a match to start the fire. Taking the coffee pot, he dumped the stale coffee into the pail below the sink, rinsed it out, added fresh water to the pot and set that on the stove top.

"Now," Rusty said, "Let's get you cleaned up, get some hot coffee or tea in you, and decide what to do. First of all, what do we call you?"

The woman rubbed her wrists; they were red and sore where the tape cut into her skin. "My name is Ruth Benson."

"And?" Max questioned, "How did you get yourself into this mess?"

"How long were you tied up in the chicken house?" wondered Rusty, noticing her wet jeans and the strong odor?

Ruth's eyes welled with tears again. "They tied me up this morning. It doesn't take much to put LeRoy in a foul mood. He said I was a worthless piece of crap and they didn't know why they should keep me around. LeRoy can be evil. He thinks he's the king pin, the one in charge. But he's not! Billy isn't so bad I think he is being controlled. I don't know what kind of a hold LeRoy has on him."

"That doesn't sound like a good enough reason to leave you tied up all day," stated Rusty.

"Tell us your story. Where did you meet these guys?" asked Max.

The water began to boil. Max poured some into a cup, plopped a tea bag in it and handed it to Ruth.

"The tea is ready," he said,

He looked at Rusty, "Or would you rather have coffee."

"Tea is fine for me too." Rusty said.

Max made two more cups and handed one to Rusty. Then he took a cookie out of the sack and passed the sack to the ladies.

Ruth answered, "I met Billy when I was in college. He wasn't a student, but he did hang out with some of the people I knew. He was fun! We went to movies and parties. It was at a party that he introduced me to drugs."

"Are you warm enough? You're shivering!" Rusty observed.

Max went into the living room and came back with an afghan and put it around her shoulders.

"Go on, what happened then?" He wanted to know.

"After a few times of getting high, I was hooked. Then Billy went to prison. He got caught passing out treats at the high school."

Rusty was appalled. "What? Getting teens hooked? What kind of a monster is he?"

"He was just doing what LeRoy ordered him to do. That's when I went to LeRoy for drugs. I had to go to work for him to support my habit. I worked out of Plains. Eventually I was caught and went to jail, but I was lucky, they put me in a rehabilitation program. I spent many weeks in a facility sweating the drugs out of my system."

Max backed up and sat on the table, "At least you're clean now."

Ruth nodded. "I sure didn't think I ever wanted to experience that again! I hurt all over, throwing up, not sleeping, the nightmares when I did fall asleep. It was awful."

"How did you end up in the barn?"

"LeRoy is a cruel man. He'd beat me! Yesterday I backslid, I didn't think one pill would hurt. I stole a couple pills when he wouldn't give me any. He knocked me unconscious. When I woke up I was in the straw chicken house, bound in duck tape. I was there for hours before you came."

Max reached for her empty cup. "How long was Billy in prison?"

"He was sentenced to five years for the first offense, but he got out in three, because of good behavior. I couldn't believe it when I saw him again. He had tattoos and looked scary."

"Max do you have a clean pair of overalls and maybe a tee shirt? I'll help Ruth get cleaned up, and then we'll take her into Plains to be checked out at the hospital!

"No, no way, I appreciate that you rescued me, but I ain't going to any hospital! Period!"

Both Max and Rusty stared at her, surprised by her outburst.

"What do you suggest we do with you then?" Rusty asked.

"Just let me go, I can take care of myself."

Rusty's mind was whirling. Her tiny house wasn't big enough for two people, but Nona's big rambling house on the edge of town was a perfect place to get things sorted out.

"It doesn't look like you can take care of yourself, would you let me bring you to my friends' house? You could take a shower, get clean clothes, and then we can decide on the next step."

"Let me call her." She noted that Max was making jelly sandwiches on the table. When he handed one to Ruth, she took her cell phone out of her pocket, stepped out onto the porch and punched a button.

"Nona, I have a problem and I need your help." Rusty went down the steps and paced around the yard while she told Nona about her afternoon. Nona was quiet and listen until she finished.

"It sounds like she needs help; I guess it would be okay. Should I call Booga?"

"Not yet, let's get her cleaned up and fed, then sort things out."

Nona agreed and Rusty went back in the house. Max was chatting away and Ruth seemed much more relaxed. She had finished her jelly sandwich and was working on another cookie.

"It's a go, my friend Nona said she'd be happy to let you use her shower and let you spend the night," Rusty lied.

Nona had just said okay to the shower. But she was sure Nona would let her spend the night if she begged and begged.

"I'll loan her some of my clothes Max, don't worry about finding something for Ruth to wear."

"I don't think I could anyway," Max replied, "This is my cleanest dirty pair of pants, I might have a tee shirt clean, I'm doing laundry when I go get groceries in a couple days."

Rusty couldn't help but chuckle; she might have known that Max didn't have a closet full of clothes.

"We better be on our way, I'll be back in a few days."

Ruth followed Rusty out the door and down the steps. She looked up at Max who had followed them unto the porch.

"Thank you Max, the tea hit the spot and the sandwich was delicious. I can't remember the last time I had a jelly sandwich, it seems like a lifetime ago."

Max waved, and watched them walk to the car.

Ruth automatically climbed into the back of the car and lay down. Rusty figured she fell asleep as all she heard was even breathing.

It was dark when Rusty pulled into Nona's driveway and drove around to the back of her house, parking so her car couldn't be spotted from the road. The back porch light glowed, lighting the stone walkway. Nona opened the door before they could ring the bell, ushering them inside, she shut and locked the door.

"Thanks Nona, I didn't know what else to do, I knew you had extra sleeping space and was hoping Ruth could spend the night."

"By the way this is Ruth Benson, the lady I was telling you about. Ruth this is my friend Nona, you probably remember her from when you have been in my shop"

Ruth looked startled. She hadn't connected the dots that it was Rusty who owned *Holly, Wood and Wine.* When she looked at Rusty and Nona, she seemed to wilt.

Oh, Crap! Ruth thought, why didn't I recognize her, of all the people living in and around Sandy Bay it had to be her who found me.

Ruth managed to mumble, "Nice to meet you."

"Let's get you cleaned up," Nona said with a smile. "I'll show you to the bathroom and we can throw your clothes in the washer. By the time your finished eating you'll have clean clothes. After a good nights sleep, you'll feel better and in the morning we can get you some help."

Ruth let Nona lead her up stairs. In the bathroom there was a pair of pajamas, bath towel, and wash cloth laying on the vanity. Nona reached down and started the water in the tub, set out the shampoo, conditioner, toothpaste and a new tooth brush.

"I'll wait in the hall, when you get undressed, just hand your dirty clothes out the door and I'll get them in the machine."

Ruth did as she was told.

Relaxing in the warm water was soothing. Ruth hadn't even realized she had been shaking until she stopped. The tears came. She cried quietly. She knew she couldn't stay here and put the lives of these women in danger.

Nona returned to the kitchen, Rusty had helped herself to a cup of coffee and was sitting at the table sipping. Nona had a quiche mixed and sitting in a bowl on the cupboard. She poured it into a pie shell and slid it into the oven. Neither said anything. It was quiet except for the washer swishing in a small room off the kitchen. After taking a loaf of bread from the refrigerator and the toaster out of the cupboard,

Nona poured herself a cup of coffee and sat down across the table from Rusty.

"Now what?" she asked.

Rusty looked at her, "I don't know!" she answered.

Whispering in case Ruth could hear her, Rusty said, "I think it's my shop that is the drug drop, but I don't know how that happened or how it works."

"We need to contact Booga;" Nona whispered back, "he'll know what needs to be done."

"I think Ruth has been abused and used, but she'll be arrested for her part in it too!"

Nona nodded, "We'll feed her, clean her up, let her rest and deal with it in the morning."

"I agree," Rusty commented, "we need to think."

The oven timer buzzed, just as Ruth appeared in the doorway.

Even though both Ruth and Nona were about the same height, Nona's pajamas were big on her. In fact the sleeves were rolled up, and she was holding the bottoms up with her left hand.

Nona smiled. "You look like your drowning in those, in fact you look like a little girl with wet hair and rosy cheeks."

Ruth couldn't help but smile.

Rusty grinned and said, "I think Ruth needs a pin to hold up the pants, she does look like she's drowning, the top almost touches her knees."

Rusty turned and put bread in the four slice toaster and said, "I'll bet your starving too! I know my stomach is fighting with my backbone. Nona made a quiche and it smells wonderful."

Pulling out a chair Nona said "Sit", and then walked over to the oven and took out the quiche. After setting it on a hot pad on the table she left to transfer Ruth's clothes from the washer to the dryer. Rusty helped by getting plates and putting them on the table. Finding another cup she poured coffee for Ruth and refilled hers and Nonas.

Conversation was light, both Rusty and Nona were careful not to mention the reason they were all together.

Ruth watched them warily and concentrated on her food. Her eyes were so heavy they kept going shut; she struggled to keep them open. After eating Nona took her upstairs and showed her where she could sleep. Rusty cleared the table, and filled the sink with water and washed the dishes.

"It didn't take her long to fall asleep." Nona commented when she returned to the kitchen.

Rusty said, "She has had a stressful day and who knows what she has been through before I found her bound and gagged in a straw shed."

Nona picked up a towel and began drying dishes, "We need to contact the police and get her some help, that won't be easy for her though, I'm sure she'll suffer the repercussions too along with whoever else is part of this ring."

Rusty agreed, and then said, "One of them, the mean one is called Le Roy, and the good crook is called Billy. That is what she told Max and Me.

Chapter 11

Rusty drove through the main street of Sandy Bay to the east side of town. The shops were closed. Dim security lights glowed in the windows. The liquor store was still brightly lit, only one car sat outside. The occupant was most likely inside making a purchase. On an impulse she went around the block to drive past her shop, everything looked good. She didn't stop. The only other business open was the gas station on the corner. That was quiet too!

Making a U-turn on the corner by the station, she headed for home and pulled up in front of her tiny house. It was 10 O'clock. Unlocking her front door, she went in and kicked off her shoes, pulled the drapes on her patio door, and sank down on the love seat.

Rusty dug in her pocket for her cell phone, looked up the number for the police station and punched it in.

Booga sounded tired. "Sandy Bay Police Department Booga here."

"Hi Booga, this is Rusty, I need to talk to you. Is this a good time?"

"Yes, what can I help you with?"

"It's a long story; I think I stumbled onto a drug ring."

The line was quiet; Rusty wondered if they'd been cut off. Then Booga answered.

"You want to come in and talk or should I come over?"

"Do you mind coming here? I'll make some coffee."

"I'll be over." The phone went dead.

Booga arrived 20 minutes later. With him was the cowboy, the man with the hat and boots, and Kevin Barker.

"Well Hello!" Rusty exclaimed in surprise. She looked from Booga to the cowboy and back at Kevin.

Booga explained, "Kevin also works with us, this is Wade; both Kevin and Wade work with the Drug Task Force from St. Paul." Rusty gawked at Kevin trying to process that while Booga took a seat on the small sofa.

Kevin smiled rather sheepishly and sat down beside him. Wade perched on a stool by the small counter that separated the kitchen from the living room. The three of them together dwarfed her tiny home.

After handing the men a cup of coffee and taking one herself she opened the patio door and brought in a folding lawn chair from the deck.

Booga took a sip of the hot liquid, and then asked "Okay, what is this all about? Maybe start from the beginning."

Rusty began, "The beginning is a man named Max." She went onto explain how she had met him and why she was on his farm.

The men listened politely while she told how her birdhouses and chests were big sellers in her store. When she got to the part in her story about Max taking her to his friend Fred's farm to take more pictures, Booga leaned forward.

"When I found Ruth in the straw shed, she was tied up behind the door, scared out of her wits and covered with urine and straw. I took Max home then called my friend Nona Baton to see if Ruth could clean up and maybe spend the night. We thought we should call Law Enforcement, but Ruth panicked. We agreed it might be a good idea to wait until morning."

"What made you decide to call tonight?" asked Wade.

"I thought you should know about it right away, and I wanted to give you the birdhouse and chest I picked up in the corner of the straw shed."

Wade set his cup on the counter and asked, "Where is this abandoned farm of Fred's?"

Rusty got up and found a pen and paper, "It's about fifteen or twenty miles north, closer to Plains. I'll draw you a map." When she was finished the men examined the crude drawing. Then Wade said, "We'll pick you up in the morning, you can take us there."

The men rose in unison and headed for the door.

Kevin stopped and turned to Rusty, "Do I still have a job in your shop?"

"Only if it is to do more surveillance," she smiled, "I'm sure you have better things to do than to clean and stock shelves." Kevin grinned and followed Wade out the door.

"Thanks for the information and the coffee," Booga said "We'll pick you up about nine." He turned and went out into the dark not waiting for an answer.

Rusty picked up the coffee cups and took them to the sink. Looking at the clock she saw it was after midnight. She felt exhausted! Shutting off the downstairs lights she felt her way to the bathroom to wash her face and brush her teeth. She climbed to the loft in the dark, the sky light in the ceiling let in just enough moonlight, and she undressed and fell into bed. Her mind was racing, trying to sort things out, tossing and turning she was sure she'd never sleep.

Her phone was ringing! At first Rusty didn't know what the noise was, thinking it was the alarm clock she reached to shut it off. Shoot! Why didn't she ever think of bringing her phone upstairs? Scrambling she half tumbled down the steps, hanging onto the rail. Her eyes darted around the room and spotted her cell on the counter. By then it had stopped ringing. Nona's voice came on voicemail. "Rusty, call me! Ruth's gone!"

Rusty punched in Nona's number and she picked up immediately.

"What do you mean Ruth's gone?" shouted Rusty.

"Don't yell in my ear. She left sometime during the night. Ruth's gone!" Nona was yelling too!

"Where did she go?"

"How should I know?"

"Nona, I called Booga last night, he came over with men from the Drug Task Force and I told them the whole story. And would you believe our Kevin works with them?"

"No way! Not Kevin who works in the shop?"

"Yes, way! I'll need to call Booga and tell him she left, maybe he can find her."

"Before I forget to ask, can you hold down the fort at the shop this morning?" Rusty continued, "I need to show them where Fred's farm is located. I'll be in as soon as I can."

"Don't worry about it, I can do that. It's Saturday so it isn't all day."

Rusty hung up, and looked up Booga's number again. You'd think she would know it by heart, but no! Booga answered on the third ring.

"Booga here!"

"This is Rusty, Nona just called; Ruth took off sometime during the night. She was gone when Nona got up this morning."

Booga didn't answer right away, then said, "I'll check the roads leading out of town, maybe I can find her if she's walking." The phone went dead.

One thing about Booga, he didn't waste words. He was blunt and to the point.

Rusty cringed; the train with the piercing whistle was chugging through town. The grain elevator was located on the west side of town; it most likely dropped some cars, or added some, during the night and was just heading east. She swore the engineer delighted in blowing the whistle extra loud and extra long when they crossed over county road 16. Nona never complained even though the grain elevator was close to her house and blew corn crap all over her yard every fall when they started up the dryers. Rusty noted the time and measured coffee into the coffee maker. It was still a couple hours before she had to act as a guide and bring the guys to Fred's farm. She had plenty of time and headed for the shower to get ready for the day.

Rusty took her coffee and toast out to the deck, the humming bird at the feeder flew away, but came back after she sat down. She saw the bird, but her mind was somewhere else. She wondered where Ruth had gone and when she had left. Brad ran by, but stopped when he saw Rusty.

"We missed you last night at cocktail hour; the park is having a potluck supper tonight. I hope you're not working late or stepping out on the town."

Rusty was so engrossed in her thoughts she hadn't noticed him until he spoke.

"What? Oh, no! Sure I'll be there."

Just then Wade and Kevin pulled up in the old blue pickup. Kevin jumped out and grinned, "Your chariot awaits." He said bowing from the waist.

Brad wasn't sure what to do, so he said, "See ya' tonight!" waved and was off running toward the lake.

"I'll grab my things and lock up, be right there."

Rusty took her cup in the house with her, locked the patio door, pulled the drapes, and picked up her belt bag; she didn't want to bother with a purse. She grabbed her sweater off the back of the love seat, and then locked the front door behind her.

"Where is Booga?" she asked looking around.

"Out looking for the woman." Wade growled, "Shoulda' went over and got her last night, instead of waiting."

Rusty crawled in the pick-up between the men, straddling the stick shift on the floor.

She asked, "Is this even legal? No seat belts? Three people in the front seat?"

"I guess it is today," said Kevin with a grin.

Wade turned the key, the truck roared to life. He reached between her legs and shifted into first gear and slowly pulled out of the park and onto the road. He seemed to enjoy embarrassing Rusty by shifting through second and third. She told him where to turn, and then no one said anything until they were speeding along the gravel road with dust flying behind them.

"Let's go over this again;" said Wade, "I just want to make sure you're an innocent by-stander and not just one disgruntled member of this ring of misfits."

Rusty felt a flash of anger, she stared at Wade, then turned and looked at Kevin.

"You don't really think I've got anything to do with this do you?"

Wade said, "I don't know you. Kevin doesn't know you. And here you are, right in the middle of an investigation we've been following for months. Now one of our own has been murdered by these jerks."

"Well, I have nothing to do with this or anything connected to it, you should know that Kevin, you've been working in my store for weeks."

Rusty's voice was hard and had an edge to it. Make no bones about it, she was mad! Kevin didn't answer, but he did look at Wade in surprise.

"I told you everything I know last night, and now I'm showing you where I found the broken birdhouses and chests. It is up to you if you believe me or not."

They drove past Max's farm. Rusty never said a word. She certainly didn't want to involve him in this mess.

"Turn left at the next corner," she instructed. But she didn't say anything else until they came to Fred's partially overgrown driveway.

Wade stopped by the same old building Rusty had stopped at yesterday. He put the truck in park and pulled out the key.

"You stay here!" he demanded. Both men got out of the pick-up, quietly shut and latched the doors.

Rusty watched as the men walk away, and when she could no longer see them, she opened the door and got out, shutting and latching the door as quietly as possible. She didn't follow them, but used the same path as Max had used when he returned from his walk in the woods.

Carefully picking her way through the high weeds, fallen branches and impossible underbrush she made her way to a place in the grove where she had a good view of the old barn and the straw chicken house. Here she discovered another road, one that seemed to be leading into a corn field. She spotted a huge Cottonwood tree. Around the trunk of the tree fence poles were stacked vertically. It looked like a teepee with a tree growing through the roof. Rusty looked around, didn't see anyone. That tree looked like as good a place as any from which to watch. When she inspected it further she discovered she could crawl into the log teepee and sit, but she couldn't see anything so she crawled out again. Then deciding to get closer to the barn, she moved through the grove as silently as possible.

Someone yelled! She could hear shouting, then swearing, and more yelling. Rusty ran toward the voices that were coming from behind the barn. Going at a dead run she rounded the building and crashed smack into someone else coming around the corner at a dead run. The person fell backwards. When all was said and done, Rusty was laying on top of a skinny man with tattoos. She looked at his face with horror. Teardrops had been tattooed in his cheeks under his eyes. New eyebrows were tattooed into devil like arches above his eyes. His skin was dull with sores; his cheeks were sunken with vertical black lines painted on his face.

Kevin was the first to reach them. He took her arm and helped her stand.

Wade grabbed the man, pulled him to his feet and cuffed him. He glared at Rusty, "I told you to stay in the truck. Don't you ever do anything your told?"

Rusty glared back! It didn't seem like a question, so she had sense enough to stay quiet.

She looked at the man in cuffs; at his raccoon style hair cut dyed in stripes and almost felt sorry for him. The tattoos alone would keep him from ever getting a decent job. He must be going through hell. Her mind was whirling. She remembered hearing that someone was making methamphetamine.

The little bit she knew about meth addiction wasn't much. She had read that meth addiction triggers a high. A release of some pleasure drug, she remembered that it was called dopamine. You had to be a dope to try it. She knew what goes up must come down, so the opposite would be intense depression. Then they take more of that horrid stuff to make that horrid feeling go away. She didn't know anyone who used drugs, but she had heard their moods are erratic and their behavior unpredictable. Why in the world would someone do that to their body?

Rusty couldn't help but stare at the man. He was also staring at her. Did she know him? No, she had never seen anyone who looked like him. She would have remembered.

Wade gave his prisoner a little push toward the driveway, Kevin followed with Rusty bringing up the rear. The druggie staggered on ahead with Wade steering him by the waist band of his pants. Rusty couldn't help but wonder how they were all going to ride back to town in a pick-up where three people in the cab were squished. She'd wait to see if Mr. Wade had any bright ideas.

He did! When they got to the truck, he put junkie in the front. He basically picked him up and set him on the seat, grabbed his legs and turned him toward the front. Then he opened the glove box and took out a roll of silver duct tape and taped his ankles together. After slamming the door, he remarked, "Just in case he decides to do any kicking."

It was then that Rusty noticed that Kevin was taking some cardboard and an old blanket out of the tool box that stretched across the back of the pick-up under the rear window. He arranged them in the bed of the truck. She had a good idea where she'd be riding back to town. She was right!

Kevin grinned holding out his hand. "Come to the back by the tailgate, I'll give you a hand up, this will be fun."

Rusty wasn't sure, but she gave him a weak smile and took his hand. She'd have an adventure to tell about tonight at the pot luck supper.

It was 11 O'clock when the pick-up stopped in front of her tiny home. She stood and stumbled to the back of the truck. Kevin hopped down first and helped Rusty climb down. Mumbling a thank you she glanced toward the cab, Wade was looking straight ahead and junkie was slouched against the window, probably sleeping.

"Oh, well," she muttered, "It is what it is!" She gave a little wave to Kevin, who waved back and climbed up into the rear of the truck. Rusty slowly walked to her house; she looked like she was sneaking up on someone. As much as she tried it hurt too much to straighten up.

A hot shower and a couple Aleve seemed to do the trick. She didn't remember ever taking two showers in one morning. She arrived to her shop a little after noon to relieve Nona.

Chapter 12

When Rusty opened the back door, she could hear laughter coming from the front of the shop. She poured her-self a cup of coffee and took a sip. It was lukewarm and very strong. She made a face, grimaced, and took it with her when she joined Nona. Rusty's neighbors Rose and Ava were at the counter paying for two bottles of wine.

"What's so funny?" Rusty asked, taking another sip of the tepid coffee.

Nona was still chuckling, "Rose got a call last night from her son, oh Rose, you tell it, if I try it'll lose something in the translation."

Rose giggled, "It went like this, and he was talking to Ernie."

"Dad, I got a damn mouse."

Ernie: "What's wrong with your cat?"

"It's useless, so I set a trap behind the fridge and baited it with a tootsie roll."

Ernie: "Hmmmm! A tootsie roll?"

"Yep! Uncle Dale, your brother, said that is how to do it."

Ernie: "That is pretty damn redneck. Did it work?"

"Nope!"

Everyone, busted out laughing again, Rusty included. Rose picked up her package, and the ladies started toward the door. Ava turned and asked, "See you tonight?"

After everything that had happen that morning Rusty hadn't thought about the potluck. "Is it OK if I bring fruit?"

"Sounds good, see you later."

After they left, Rusty asked, "Have you had a busy morning Nona?"

"Not too busy, people were dropping in, not a lot of packages went out, but they did a lot of looking. How did your morning go?"

Rusty didn't know how much she should share; she didn't want to jinx the investigation. She was sure the other people that were involved didn't know that the police had arrested one of them.

"I showed them where Fred's farm was, Wade and Kevin walked around and I stayed out of the way." A little white lie wouldn't hurt. *I'll tell her more when everything cools down.*

"I did have an interesting ride home though; Kevin and I rode home in the back of the pick up."

Nona was walking toward the back room, but stopped. Turning back she commented. "Cool! Is that even legal anymore? As kids we did that a lot. But now everyone needs to be in a seat belt."

Rusty smiled, shrugged her shoulders, cocked one eyebrow, and didn't answer her question.

"Would you like to have the afternoon off Nona? We close at two and you were here alone all morning, I can take over if you want to go home."

"Sure if you don't need me, I've got some weeding to do and I could practice the piano for church in the morning."

Rusty dumped the terrible coffee down the drain, washed the pot and dirty cups, swept the floors and called it a day. Her back ached and she was feeling drained. Before she could close out the till a mother with her two young daughters came through the door and began browsing. They left with a small stuffed teddy bear and a pair of Lake Superior Agate earrings.

What a morning. She couldn't help but think about the young man, high on drugs and full of tattoos. Her stomach felt like it was turning somersaults, she just felt jittery. After locking the doors and setting the alarm, she stopped at the grocery store and picked up a watermelon for the potluck.

Pulling into her driveway, she saw Jessie was weeding her flowers. She looked up when she heard the car and waved. Rusty returned the greeting, took the watermelon, her purse, unlocked her front door, and set the melon on the counter. Sighing she walked across the room, picked up the remote and turned on the TV. Punching in number 950 country music blasted out of the set. She turned it down. Then off. Lying down on the love seat, she closed her eyes. After reliving the morning, she could hardly believe it wasn't a dream. No wonder her head hurt.

Banging on the door woke her; she sat up, and then staggered to open the door. It was Brad. "Are you coming? We were wondering if you were home. Jessie said you were, but then thought you might have left for a walk."

"I fell asleep," Rusty answered, she felt groggy, "I'll be right there. Are you out back or by the lake?"

"By the lake, can I carry something?" Rusty opened the door to let him enter.

"Sure, grab the watermelon and a knife and I'll be right there." She repeated.

Brad left; Rusty went into the bathroom and splashed cold water on her face.

Man, she thought, I never nap; I don't know what came over me. I must have been really tired.

Fifteen minutes later Rusty showed up at the dock by the lake with her glass and small bottle of wine. Everyone was there but her.

"Here she comes, Sleeping Beauty," said Bruce.

Rusty stuck out her tongue at him.

Bruce laughed, a hearty laugh, it came from somewhere deep down. She guessed the beer he was holding wasn't the first one.

Brad had cut the watermelon and the slices were sitting on a white plastic garbage bag on top of news paper.

"Love your serving platter Brad," Rusty stated.

"Well, it works!" He said with a grin, "Let's eat!"

Trina pushed Bruce out of the way and stepped in front of him, quickly grabbing the plate he was about to take.

"The way to a man's heart is through his stomach," he joked, "your not making any points with my heart."

"He that is of merry heart hath a continual feast." Trina quipped in return.

Bruce was a confirmed bachelor in his early 60's, he sported a small mustache. Being a career military man, he seemed to always be standing at attention, tall and straight. Normally he was quiet and reserved; tonight his brown eyes were dancing with merriment. Trina being a good 10 years his junior wasn't about to take any of his guff.

The sun was sinking beneath the lake; a fire had been built on the beach. Conversation was low, everyone was full and relaxed.

A train went through town, the whistle piercing the stillness of the night. Glen looked at his watch.

"It's that time," he said, "I wonder if there is anything different on the ten o'clock news. Are you ready to go Ava?"

Ava stood and folded her lawn chair. She gave it to Glen to carry. Collecting her left over potato salad, she called loudly, "Good night everyone,"

"Good night to you too," the group called in unison.

Ernie yawned and stood up, "Good night all, I'm going to hit the hay too, coming Rose?"

Bruce and Brad put the fire out. The neighbors began to collect their bowls and depart for their tiny houses.

Rusty and Trina waited for Brad and they walked to the east end of the park together.

Rusty had left the light on in the kitchen so she didn't have to go into a dark house. The light shone out onto the small porch. She climbed the steps and stopped short. Written on the glass window of the door with a black marker, was one word. "BITCH!"

Taking a step backwards, she paused, and looked toward Trina's house. The light came on in the kitchen. Rusty was off her porch and across the yard in a flash. Knocking on Trina's door she called, "Trina open the door!" The door swung open, Trina stood, still holding her bowl of leftover coleslaw.

"Good grief Rusty, what's the matter?"

"Can I use your phone? I need to call Booga. While we were at the lake someone has been at my house and wrote "Bitch" on the door."

Trina set her bowl down and handed her cell phone to Rusty. Passing the plastic bag of left over melon to Trina she said, "I left my phone on the counter, there is no way I'm going into the house alone."

"Shoot! I never remember his number; do you have a phone book?"

Trina grabbed the book out of the cupboard drawer and opened it to the front page where the emergency numbers were listed. Rusty punched in the numbers as Trina read 431-675-0304. The phone rang, and rang, and rang. No answer. Dang! Punching off, she remembered Kevin's cell phone number and quickly dialed that. He answered on the second ring.

"Hi, I'm Kevin, what are you?"

"Kevin, this is Rusty, I'm sorry to bother you at this time of the night, but I just came home and someone was here while I was gone and wrote "Bitch" on my door."

"Where are you now?"

"At the neighbors, I'm not going in the house alone."

"That's smart. Just hang tight, I'm coming. You know you really should get a dog."

Rusty didn't answer; she clicked off and handed the phone back to Trina.

"Can I get you something to drink while we're waiting? A glass of water?" asked Trina.

"No, thanks, I'm too nervous to drink anything." Rusty paced in circles around in the tiny kitchen.

"How did you remember Kevin's cell number and not Boogas." Trina wondered.

"Kevin has been working at the store for a few weeks; I've had to call him on a couple occasions. His cell number is mine backwards. That is how I remember."

Ten minutes later the old blue pick-up pulled up in front of her house. Wade, Booga and Kevin got out and stood looking at the door.

Rusty said "Thanks again Trina," and went to join them. Trina followed her, now her curiosity was peaked; she had to know was happening.

Booga returned to the truck and removed a plastic case. Rusty watched him open it and saw some cards, powder, and brush along with other items. She knew why he hadn't answered his phone. His eyes had a glazed look and he smelled of booze. Kevin took Rusty by the arm and led her and Trina away from the door.

"Let's get out of their way while they work," He said with a grin.

"Soooo, Bitch? You're not a female dog, a wolf or an otter. You must be a fox. Yes, that's it, you're a fox."

Rusty gave him a faint smile. Trina had her back to them still watching the men by the door. She half turned to Rusty.

"Are you in some kind of trouble? This is scary. When you got the flowers and candy we thought you had a secret admirer, now I'm not so sure. It seems more like a dangerous stalker."

"Trina, I'd like to tell you what's going on, but I don't know myself. It is just weird!"

Wade was walking around the house with a flashlight. He came back with a cigarette filter pinched in a tweezers.

"Kevin, see if there is a baggy in the glove box of the truck."

Booga was finished too. "How do you feel about staying here tonight? I think you'll be fine, but I want to check inside first."

Rusty reached into her pocket and handed Booga the keys. Kevin came back with the bag. Wade dropped the filter in the bag and zipped it shut. Booga handed Kevin the plastic box before he and Wade went into the house.

A few minutes later they returned, Wade said, "It's an all clear. It doesn't look like anyone has been in the house. Make sure the doors are locked and the alarm is set. I'll take these to the lab in Plains. We should have the results in a couple of days."

Wade and Booga climbed into the pick-up. Kevin saluted and hopped in the back. They waited until Rusty and Trina were both in doors before driving away.

Chapter 13

Rusty stretched and rolled over onto her back. She saw the bright blue sky through the skylight. She had opened the window a crack last night, now she stood on the bed, cranked it shut and turned the lock. She didn't think anyone would climb up on her slanted roof to break in, but she wasn't taking any chances. Her cell phone rang; she reached over, picked it up off the floor, and lay back down.

"Hello?"

"Hey there, how are you doing this morning?"

She recognized Kevin's voice. "I don't feel like I slept a wink last night. What are you doing up already, it's Sunday."

"I always get up early. I figured it was late enough to check on you, its 8 o'clock. What are your plans for today?"

"Well, my stomach is still doing flips and I feel a little jumpy. Keeping things as normal as possible is what my plan is for today."

124

"That sounds like a great idea. Rest and relaxation!"

After a little more small talk, she hung up the phone and headed downstairs. Looking closely in the mirror she tried to smooth out the bags under her eyes. Grinning at herself, she studied her teeth. Running her fingers through her auburn hair, she reached for the shampoo, turned on the water and stepped into the shower.

Thirty minutes later the coffee was dripping and the toast popped up. She opened the sliding glass door and stepped out onto the deck. She loved sitting there in the morning thinking about her day and eating her breakfast. She had dressed in a totally inappropriate shade of pink, it clashed with her reddish hair and she didn't even care. Instead of walking to church Rusty decided to drive. Then she'd drive out to see Max. She needed gas in the car; she could pick up something for lunch at the convenience store. Maybe she and Max could have a picnic. Rusty felt a little better having her day planned.

The pastor told a story before his sermon this morning that really seemed to hit home. It was a story about an old man leading a donkey with a young man on its back. As they traveled they soon heard, "look at that poor old man walking and that strapping young man riding the donkey."

So the old man rode and the young man led the donkey.

Then they heard, "look at that able bodied man riding the donkey and that poor boy is walking."

So they both walked and led the donkey. "Look at that fine donkey not being ridden, it is such a waste. No one is using it."

So they both rode the donkey and they heard, "That poor donkey, see how hard it's working."

Both the man and boy riding the donkey got off and the old man carried the donkey.

The moral of this story is that people always find something to complain about. You're damned if you do and your damned if you don't.

That story made an impression. She would remember it longer than the than she'd remember the sermon.

A couple hours later Rusty turned onto the gravel road leading out to the farm. It was a nice day, sunny with a slight breeze. She slowed for a pair of Canada Geese strolling along the road by the bridge, and decided it was a pretty day for both a drive in the country and a picnic. When Rusty turned into the driveway she saw Max's old car parked outside the garage and pulled in behind it. Max was sitting on a tree stump inside the garage. He looked pleased when he saw Rusty; she waved and slammed the car door.

"What are you doing Max?" she asked walking into the garage.

"Carving a top! Just putting the finishing touches on it." He set the top on a board and gave it a spin. They both watched it spin, slow down, wobble and fall.

Rusty laughed. "Can I try that?"

Max picked it up and handed it to her. "It's yours."

"Thanks!" She said inspecting the carving and running her fingers over the smooth wood.

After a few tries, she had it spinning crazily on the board.

"This is good Max, it's a cool toy. Would you mind making a few of these for the shop?"

Max blushed and lowered his head. "I guess I could! It'd give me something to do."

"How do you feel about picnics?"

"Haven't been on one for years," he answered, "don't know how I feel about 'em."

"I picked up food, do you know a place?"

Max thought a minute, "There is a place, Fred and I used to go there when we were young and out hunting gophers. Back then they would pay you for shootin' 'em. Could be bugs though, it's by a marsh."

"I've got bug spray!" She quipped. "I'll drive you tell me where to go."

Max started his old car and pulled it into the garage. Rusty helped him shut the big doors.

"I bought some baby chicks at the farm store in Plains, fifteen of them. Come see, I need to shut the door so no wild critters get in and eat 'em."

Rusty followed Max to what he called the brooder house. Peering around him she could see he had an old screen window covering the bottom half of the door.

"I couldn't make up my mind which I should get, so I got a few of every color." He chuckled. "It will make for an interesting flock." He added proudly.

Rusty and Max stood admiring the yellow, brown, and black baby chicks.

"They are really cute; you'll be pretty busy taking care of them."

"Yep, gives me a reason to get up in the morning."

He moved the screen to the side, shut and latched the door.

Soon they were tooling down the gravel road at 25 miles an hour.

They turned left and went past Fred's place.

"It's just a little farther, Fred and I used to walk or take the horses. We'd let them graze while we hunted, then ride 'em home."

"Sounds like an interesting childhood."

"Oh, we worked too, it wasn't all play. Our fathers saw to that. We didn't bale hay in the 40's we shocked hay, threw them on a hayrack and took them to the thresher. We'd milk cows at five in the morning and five at night. There were barns to clean, manure to haul; we carried water, lots of water. Yep, them were the good ole' days."

"It doesn't sound all that good! But that's probably why you're still in such good shape today, all that exercise helped."

"Well, we had a lot of freedom too, just needed to finish our chores. Here we are! Pull into this approach we'll have to walk from here."

Rusty gave Max a plastic bag with drinks and he left following the line fence alongside a corn field. Rusty picked up the other bag holding the food. She grabbed the bug spray, locked the doors, and trailed after Max. He was doing a lot better walking through the weeds than Rusty. Sand burrs were sticking to her black canvas shoes and socks; she noticed Max had stuck his pant legs into the tops of his boots.

Five minutes later they came to another fence. On the other side she could see the grassy meadow surrounding the marsh.

"Ahhhhh! Now what?" Rusty asked, hoping they hadn't walked way out here for nothing.

"No worries," Max replied, "I'll hold the fence for you, you hold it for me! Set your bag on the ground," he suggested.

Stepping on the bottom two rows of barbed wire he held the top one up for Rusty to climb through.

"Are you going to be able to crawl through Max?"

"We'll soon find out, now you go through first."

Rusty held the fence for Max. She was surprise to see how agile he was for eighty something. He did catch the back pocket of his bibbed overalls on the barb and ripped a small hole. Max led the way to a big boulder close to the marsh.

"I'd get that bug spray out about now." He grinned as he waved his arms shooing the bugs. "This is called the Minnesota wave." He laughed, "Oh, I haven't had this much fun in years."

Rusty looked unsure, she wasn't convinced that this was much fun. But she was happy that Max was happy. They began emptying the bags and setting the pop, chips, and deli chicken sandwiches on the rock. Rusty hadn't thought to grab something to sit on so they sat in the grass and began to eat.

Red wing black birds were fluttering among the bulrushes and cattails that grew in the marsh. They watched in the silence and listened as a choir of insects serenaded them.

"Are you going to shave again Max or let your beard grow?"

Before he could answer, they heard a loud boom.

"Holy Crap!" Rusty shouted, "What was that?"

"Don't know! Sounds like it came from Fred's place."

They both looked in the direction of the sound. It was all quiet. Even the birds were still.

"Well, whatever it was we'll probably never know."

Max began to chuckle, and then he laughed out loud.

Rusty was puzzled and looked at him like he had lost his mind.

"You all right?" she questioned.

"Just thinking about the time Fred and I blew up a rat hole. It sounded a lot like that."

"Go ahead," she encouraged, "I enjoy a good story."

Max took a bite of his sandwich and chewed. His brown eyes were sparkling as he thought back to his teen years.

"Well, it goes like this, Fred and I found a hole in his yard not too far from the house. We knew it was some kind of an animal. So we watched! It turned out to be a big rat. Probably came up from the Marsh to help himself to lunch in the granary and decided to stay. We set out to shoot it! We saw it, but couldn't shoot it because his mother had some kind of a lady's club at the house. So we waited. The rat was still hanging around after they left, but now a farmer had driven up and was talking to his dad. So we waited. After he left the rat was still there, Fred shot it right through the head. It was a good shot. Then we figured there might be more rats in the hole, so we stuffed the dead one back in the hole as far as we could push it in. It was getting close to the 4th of July and we had some fireworks in the garage. Taking a good sized stick we shoved that in the hole and lit it, and BANG! No kidding! The ground rose up into a nice round mound and went back down again. The whole house shook. Fred's Mom had been washing her hair, she flew out of the house, her head full of soap, suds running down her face, she was yelling and her eyes were as big as stove lids. His dad came running out of the barn with the pitchfork. Needless to say we were in a world of hurt."

Rusty was laughing so hard tears were running down her cheeks. So was Max.

Rusty blew her nose on a napkin and said, "Let's clean up and head back. I bought us each a candy bar for desert. Coffee would go good with chocolate."

Max begins stuffing wrappings into the bag, "I smell smoke," he stood up, "there's a fire! I see flames shooting up above the trees. I think Fred's house is on fire!"

They watched as tongues of fire shot toward the sky.

"My cell phone is in the car. Let's go!"

It seemed to take forever to climb the fence and wade through the grass. Unlocking the door, Rusty grabbed her phone off the dash and dialed 911. Someone answered immediately.

"I'd like to report a fire, but just a minute." She handed the phone to Max, "here you give directions to the farm."

Rusty started the car and backed back onto the road.

It didn't take long to get to Fred's; they stopped on the road to wait for the fire trucks. "Wow" said Max in amazement; "look at how quick the fire spread. Who's that running toward the barn?"

"How did Booga get out here so fast?" She exclaimed.

"Who's Booga?" Max asked.

"He's the police officer in Sandy Bay; he is investigating some drug traffic along with a couple men from the Drug Task Force. Ruth left during the night when she was staying with my friend Nona. He was searching for her; maybe that is why he is out here."

"I hear sirens, they're coming, don't see 'em yet though."

"I think I see them, the dust is flying."

Rusty started the car and backed down the road to get out of the way.

"They brought the tankers out from Plains."

Rusty answered, "Sandy Bay has one too, and they should be coming."

After the trucks pulled into the yard Rusty and Max got out of the car and walked up the driveway to watch. There is something hypnotizing about a fire. The firemen worked feverishly, but more to contain the fire than to put it out.

The tanker from Sandy Bay arrived along with the old blue pick up driven by Wade. Kevin saw Rusty and Max and walked over to join them.

"Well so much for keeping things normal! Did you call the fire in?"

"Yes, Max and I were having a picnic, there was a boom and ten minutes later fire was flaring above the trees."

"Max, this is Kevin, he is a friend, an employee, and with the Drug Task Force. Kevin, this is my friend Max."

Kevin smiled and offered his hand. Max took it and nodded his head.

Wade glanced their way and walked over to talk to the firemen.

"Did you see anyone when you got here?"

"Just Booga, he was running toward the barn when we stopped on the road. I don't think he saw us though or he would have come over to the car."

"Hmmmm! Well any evidence left in the house is gone now."

Wade was striding toward them looking as grumpy as ever.

"Does he ever smile?" wondered Rusty.

Kevin chuckled, "Not much!"

Wade greeted them with, "You're right in the middle of things again. How do you do it?"

Rusty was sure it was meant just for her, so she responded, "Your lucky we were here to call 911." Then added, "Well, Booga was here, I guess he would have called."

Wade was surprised, "He's here? I haven't been able to find him all morning. Did you see where he went?"

"He ran toward the barn."

Both Wade and Kevin started for the barn, and then Kevin returned.

"Maybe you and Max should leave, thanks for calling this in, but there's no reason for you to stay."

Rusty looked at Max, she wanted to stay. Max wanted to stay and watch. But Kevin had basically told them to get the heck out of there.

"Max and I were going to do chocolate and coffee, so I guess we should be on our way."

Kevin nodded, "See you later, I'll call." He waited until Rusty and Max walked toward her SUV then followed in the direction that Wade had taken.

"I do believe we've been nicely kicked off my friend's farm." Max exclaimed.

"I think your right, let's go get chocolate."

When they got to Max's farm, Rusty turned up the driveway and parked by the garage. "Maybe, you'd like a cup of green tea instead of coffee to go with our chocolate."

"That's a great idea, I haven't had tea for a long while, and it would taste good."

Max went into the house to make tea, and Rusty sat down on the top step. She looked across the weedy yard at the sagging barn. She noted that the door to the hay mow had been tied shut. It wasn't hanging open anymore.

Soon the door slammed and Max was standing over her holding two mugs of hot water, each had a string dangling over the top.

Rusty smiled and reached for one, and Max joined her on the step. Setting her mug down, she took a Three Musketeer bar out of the bag and handed it to Max.

"I can't remember when last I've had one of these!" He remarked as he took the candy bar with his free hand and

136

tore the paper off with his teeth. Taking a bite, he smiled with his mouth full, "Yummy."

Rusty delighted in watching him enjoying the chocolate. She sure enjoyed hers, she was a chocoholic.

Finally Max said, "Sure is sad, Fred's house going up in smoke. I'm glad he's not here to see it. There's a lot of memories in that ole' house."

"It is sad, Max, but no one was hurt. It's a good thing we were out there to call it in; otherwise all the buildings and the grove could have burned."

They sat in silence drinking their tea, each deep in thought.

Finally Rusty said, "I should get back to town Max. Thank you for the tea, and the picnic. Again, I'm so sorry about Fred's house."

Max nodded his head. He got up when Rusty did and walked with her to the car.

"I'll get working on those tops for you. You want 'em painted? I've got a couple small cans of lead free paint."

"That would be great!" Rusty responded. "I'll come back soon."

Rusty backed out of the driveway and turn onto the road. When she reached the corner, she stopped and looked toward Fred's place. Black smoke was still rising above the trees, but she didn't see any flames. She turned toward town, still thinking about the fire. There wasn't any other traffic on the road. Then out of no where a black car pulled up behind her. Glancing down she saw the needle of her speed-o-meter wavering at 45 mph. She pressed on the gas pedal to speed up; the black car pulled up along side her SUV. It didn't pass but just stayed with her inching closer and closer. She tried to see who was driving, but the windows were tinted, it was impossible to tell if it was a man or a woman. Trying to control her car took most of her concentration. When she slowed down the black car slowed. The driver was trying to run her off the road. Instinct took over and she slowed even more, turned the wheel and drove into the ditch. She had no choice. If she hadn't she would have rolled. The black car sped up and left her in a cloud of dust.

Rusty drove in the ditch and then when it wasn't so steep she drove up into a meadow. Bumping along she came to an approach and followed that back onto the road. She stopped. No one was in sight. Her hands were shaking so badly it took two tries to put the shift back into drive. Her left leg kept jerking until she put one hand on her leg and held it still. She was still trembling when she pulled up to her house.

Chapter 14

Rusty woke up at 2:30 in the morning for no apparent reason except to use the bathroom. Returning to bed she tossed and turned. Finally turning on the lamp she picked up her Patricia Cromwell paper back. Her mind kept wandering back to the fire, Booga, Ruth, and the Drug Task boys. Try as she might to make sense of everything that had happened the past month or so she could not. Some how she felt everything was related.

"What would you do Dr. Kay Scarpetta?" She asked of Cromwell's protagonist or of no one in particular. Finally she got up, showered and got ready for work.

Grey clouds hung over Sandy Bay in the early morning light. When she took her coffee and toast out onto the deck the air felt heavy and humid. Sparrows were nervously grabbing seeds out of Trina's bird feeder next door. A robin was sneaking grape jelly out of a cup that she had set out for the orioles.

"I wonder if that is the same robin that sings every morning at 4:30." She muttered.

Rusty drove to work and parked behind her shop. It began to rain just before she got her door unlocked. Quickly ducking through the door, she punched in the security code disarming the alarm. She started the coffee, turned on the computers and then went to check her shelves. Since the drugs had been found in the chests and bird houses, those she had on the shelves and in the back room had been confiscated. So she had only one wooden shelf and placqs, there were two, one said "Faith" and the other said "Peace." It would be impossible to hide anything on those.

Hearing the back door open and close, she looked at the clock and thought, "Wow! Nona is coming in early this morning. We don't open till 9 O'clock."

When Nona didn't come into the front of the store, Rusty went into the back room. At first she didn't see anyone, and then she saw Ruth crouched on the floor, in the corner outside the office door. She was drenched. Her hair hung wet and straight. Her shirt and jeans were caked with mud.

"Please you have to help me, I don't know where else to go."

"For heavens sake Ruth, where have you been? Booga's out looking for you."

"That's who I'm running away from. He's not who you think he is."

Just then the door opened again and it was Kevin.

Ruth sank back against the wall, she looked pale and defeated.

"It's okay Ruth, relax." He gave her his Kevin grin. "I'm not going to hurt you."

Rusty looked from one to another, "What is going on? Ruth where have you been? Kevin what are you doing?"

Kevin said something, but she didn't hear, because that darn train with the piercing whistle was leaving town.

When it passed Kevin said, "I'm here because I can't quit without a two week notice."

Before Rusty could answer, Ruth said quietly, "You may not need two weeks; I'm ready to tell you everything I know."

"Actually, I think we know quite a bit already. Booga's locked up in a cell in Plains. They found a body in the house that burned. DNA won't be back on that, but they are sure its LeRoy.

When Booga was being questioned, he chirped like a canary, and told us everything in exchange to do his time in a high risk facility. When a police officer commits a federal crime, he goes to prison with other inmates. However, he'll be assessed. If there is a high risk of him being attack, he'll be put in a cell or pod with other inmates with a high risk of being attack.

Booga has been looking the other way and taking a kick back from drug sales for the past three years. Then Fred died. When they saw that farm house was empty, they moved onto the farm.

Booga admitted to killing LeRoy and starting the house on fire. They still need to check and make sure it is LeRoy.

When the gas barrel ignited, that was the boom you heard." He said looking at Rusty. "We suspect that Booga lit the fire. Wade has known all along that there was someone inside the justice system covering for these guys. He figured it was Booga, but darn, he is so likeable and acts so innocent."

The back door opened again, this time it was Nona. She looked around and was surprised to see Ruth. "What's going on? Hi, you came back."

"Hi Nona, I'm glad your here, I have a favor to ask, would you mind if we take Ruth back to your house to shower? Maybe we could wash and dry her clothes. This time I'm going along so she doesn't jump a train and leave town."

"Is that what you did?" Both Rusty and Nona spoke at once looking at Ruth with surprise.

"That's what she did!" Kevin stated. "Let's get you cleaned up, then were going to Plains so you can answer some questions."

He turned to Rusty, "The only thing we can't figure out is who left the roses, candy, note, and little message on your door. But I'd ask the teacher neighbor if he can shine a light on that subject." He smiled, "No pun intended."

"I'm positive Brad doesn't know anything about it or he would have said something. So that is still a mystery." Rusty answered.

"And Kevin, yesterday when I was driving home from Max's, someone in a black car ran me off the road. I couldn't tell who it was because all the windows were tinted. They definitely did it on purpose. Someone is out to get me."

That got everyone's attention. They were all looking at her.

Kevin said, "I'll pass that along to Wade. He has a lot more experience than I, but you really need to get a dog."

Rusty heard the front door rattle. She looked at her watch.

"Oooops! Its 9 O'clock," she said heading for the door. Nona, Kevin, and Ruth headed out the back door.

A young mother stood under an umbrella trying to shield her two children from the pouring rain.

Stepping into the store the mother exclaimed, "Whoooo! It wasn't raining this hard at the camp ground when we left. It's really coming down."

Ruth was about to comment when the young boy chimed in, "Ya! It's like someone is pouring piss out of a boot."

"Clayton!" his mother scolded loudly.

"Well, that's what Grandpa said."

"I know that, but it's not nice, you don't say that!" She said sharply.

Water was dripping off the now closed umbrella.

Rusty could hardly keep a straight face, "Well now, let me take your wet umbrella. I just made a pot of coffee would you like a cup while you browse?" She said standing the umbrella in the corner.

"Yes, that would be nice, thank you."

Rusty reached for the little boys hand, "come Clayton, let's find mommy some coffee, I have something to show you."

Rusty poured the coffee, handed it to the Mom, and then led Clayton to the counter. She picked up the top that Max carved, set it on the floor and gave it a spin. Clayton watched as it spun, wobbled and fell. He looked at Rusty with shining eyes and smiled. Then he tried spinning the top. With a little coaching from Rusty he soon got the hang of it. The top spun round and round, wobbled and fell.

"How old are you Clayton?" she asked.

Clayton was busy with the top, but held up five fingers.

The little girl held up three fingers, "me tree."

Rusty smiled at her, "What is your name honey?"

"Beth, me tree." She answered.

Rusty wondered what she had for her, and then remembered one of her suppliers had brought in some clothes pin dolls.

She took Beth's little hand, and led her to a shelf. "Let's see if we can find something for you."

She took down a box and let her choose. Beth reached in and took a doll that had yellow yarn for hair, pipe cleaner arms, and a cute little face painted on the round head. Beth lifted the pink flowered dress. "Shoes," she said, pointing to the bottom of the clothes pin that had been painted black.

Beth ran away to show mommy who stood at the counter with a braided rug and a bottle of wine.

The afternoon flew by, it drizzled all day. The streets of Sandy Bay were busy with people coming into town from the campground. Shopping was a better alternative to sitting in a damp tent or camper. Many of the fishermen were in the bakery drinking coffee and eating pastries waiting while their wives checked out the shops.

Shortly before closing, three ladies came into the shop. The one with a red tee shirt was holding her jacket over her head. The other two were squeezed under an umbrella.

"This is horrid weather, we finally get away for a week and this is what we get." The red tee shirt lady complained, "doesn't matter to my husband, he would sleep in that boat if he could."

Her friend answered, "I'm really surprised the men came with us into town."

"Well, they love the doughnuts at the bakery," The red tee shirt said with a laugh.

The lady holding the umbrella addressed Rusty, "Does this town have plans for the fourth of July? You know like a parade, a community picnic, or any thing like that?"

Rusty answered, "No, but in the evening the city sponsors a fireworks display over the lake that's pretty spectacular. People come from neighboring towns to watch."

"It's just as well," the lady with the umbrella mumbled to the red tee shirt. "I know your irrational fear of port-a-potties and it would be a catastrophe should you have to use one."

"How come you're afraid of them?" the third lady asked. Then stated, "You're afraid of so many things I can't keep track. Is it the germs?"

"Nah, I have sanitizers, germs have a purpose."

The lady with the umbrella said, "Is it the germs on the floor your worried about?"

"Nah, I have shoes and will walk across the grass, just to be safe. Nope! Okay, I'll tell you what I'm afraid of, but you can't laugh."

"We won't," the two ladies said in unison.

"Well, as I'm hovering, I'm worried about the blue, gooey, liquid stuff. Has it ever? In true horror fashion? Come bubbling out of the hole and dragged someone into the blue gooey abyss of bodily fluids and single ply toilet paper?"

The third lady looked at red tee shirt with distain. "That is a slightly irrational thought process lady. More rational would be, is that someone may knock it over with you inside and you're trapped."

Red tee shirt lady shuddered, "I don't fear that, but it would suck massively."

Rusty just stood and listened in awe. When the threesome left they had bought some pottery bowls, 3 bottles of wine, and a stressed garden gate.

Rusty had ordered sparklers for the fourth of July; people were buying them for their own celebrations. It was a fairly safe way the kids could celebrate. They'd run around twirling them in the dark. Before the three ladies left she had also sold them 3 boxes of sparklers.

The last customer walked out the door at five o'clock. Rusty locked the front door. Kevin came in the back door. He pursed his lips and tried to look sad. Then he grinned. "Just wanted to tell you the case is closed and we are heading back to the cities tonight. I wanted to say thanks for the job. If I didn't enjoy what I was doing so much, I'd love to continue to work for you."

Rusty chuckled, "I'm sure that your current job pays better than I did."

Kevin started for the door.

Rusty ordered, "Hey, you come back and sit down. I have a right to know what went down."

Kevin laughed, "I was going to tell you anyway, I just wanted to know what you'd do if I pretended to leave."

He walked to the coffee pot, "Is this still warm? I could sure use a cup." He felt the pot and said, "Warm enough." He poured himself some, he looked at Rusty, and she shook her head no.

Rusty took a chair at one end of the small table and Kevin sat across from her. "First of all, your husband William isn't dead. He isn't your husband either."

Rusty looked shocked and opened her mouth to speak.

"Don't say anything." Kevin continued, "Let me tell you what we know. He is in custody as we speak; he'll be transferred to Plains tonight. They stopped him on I-90, he was traveling east at 95 miles per hour. When they checked his license, something wasn't adding up, the name on his driver's license said, Conrad Erickson. No one by that name was registered. So he was taken in for questioning. He was using a fake driver's license and he had no registration for the car. You'll be interested to know he was driving a black Mustang."

Rusty was about to say something.

Kevin shook his head, "uhah".

"William has another family in Dallas; they knew him as Benjamin. He faked a death there as well, to get away from them. After he left his boat afloat in the middle of the lake, he traveled to south Texas where he has been dealing drugs for the past 15 years. He never used the drugs himself, but he'd supply the dealers."

"Did you know he has an off shore account in the Cayman's?"

Rusty shook her head and replied, "Don't all crooks have an off shore account in the Cayman Islands?"

Kevin ignored her and went on, "The old man who made your chests and birdhouses had no clue his crafts were being used to transfer drugs to dealers. His neighbor's son was to deliver them to your shop. And he would after he stopped at Fred's farm and the drugs had been hidden in the items. By the way, he's been picked up too!"

He continued. "Your shop became a distribution point. You didn't know that the money they paid for the items with was counterfeit. The bank discovered it right away and notified the authorities. We knew it was coming from your shop and asked the bank to help by not saying anything. The Drug Task Force didn't do anything either as they needed to get the people in charge. They are in Texas. Some have been arrested; however the ones we really wanted to catch crossed into Mexico and went into hiding. William would come back here from time to time. I'm sure it wasn't easy to keep from being recognized."

Rusty sat in stunned silence, Kevin continued.

"They sold all kinds of drugs, but the methamphetamine production was at Fred's farm.

They didn't start that part of their business until they were sure no kin would be poking around.

Booga became involved after accidentally stumbling onto the operation a couple years back. Then he took a bribe to look the other way. That is why Booga had to burn the house, to destroy evidence. He shot LeRoy for a couple of reasons. The main one being LeRoy was leaving after Billy got caught and he hadn't paid Booga for services rendered. Booga was caught with 3#'s of methamphetamine. That is 1,524 ounces. It sold for $1200 an ounce. They sold it in small increments to make more money. Booga had about $100,000 on him beside the drugs. We caught him in the barn just before he was going to skip."

Rusty got up and paced around the back room. "I'll be darn, it makes sense now. William encouraged me to buy this shop. He even helped me get a loan with the same bank that loaned me money for the house. I never gave it a second thought when he didn't want his name on the loan or the building."

She repeated, "I'll be darn. He had this all planned out; him and whoever he works for." Then she asked, "What's going to happen to Ruth?"

"Right now she's in custody, but I think the judge will go easy on her. She was as much a victim as anyone. We haven't learned how she became involved, but LeRoy is a vicious man and she was under his control."

"Who killed the federal agent?"

Kevin stood up and carried his cup to the sink. "Booga followed him out of the bakery that morning and trailed him out to Fred's farm. Small town police officers don't pull in a big income and he didn't want him messing with his little gold mine. He zapped him with a taser at the farm. LeRoy came out of the house and said he'd take care of him. Booga claims he left and didn't know what happened after that. He told authorities that Agent Tom Miller was getting too close. He figured it was LeRoy and William who strung him up. Tom's a big man; he had a big lump on his head. They couldn't have overpowered him unless he was ambushed. We'll know more if William talks, but they must have had to knocked him unconscious and then put the rope around his neck."

"Wade is waiting for me at the hotel, I have to go, and I hope you'll be okay after hearing all this."

Rusty looked up at him and said boldly, "It's a lot to think about. But I'm a survivor, it's all good." She didn't feel a bit brave.

Kevin walked to the door, stopped and turned. "Oh, it was William messing with you. He gave you the roses, candy, and note. He even wrote "Bitch" on the door. The cigarette butt Wade found was Booga's."

Rusty sat down, "How did he get in the house?"

"I almost forgot," he reached into his pocket and laid a key on the counter. "William still had the key, remember you lived together in that house before he drowned." Then he added, "You should change the code to your alarm, he still remembers your birthday."

Kevin walked back to Rusty, took her hands and pulled her to her feet and gave her a big hug, then walked out the door.

Rusty felt weak and drained. "What a day!"

William was alive, but he wasn't William, he was Benjamin. She had already grieved for him. What a waste. All she felt now was anger.

"I'm so glad he is in jail. What a jerk!" She shouted, feeling angrier at herself for falling for his lies.

Rusty stood by cupboard a few more minutes, and then out of nowhere a sob escaped her lips. Tears streamed down her cheeks. She sank down by the table, laying her head in her arms she cried. Gut wrenching sobs! When the storm passed she raised her head, she felt empty. Getting up she found a clean cloth, washed her face, locked the shop and went home.

Rusty saw some of the neighbors were by the pergola; she didn't want to talk to anyone just yet. But they saw her.

Jake yelled, "Rusty, come meet our daughter and her husband."

Rusty called, "In a bit, I'll be over in a bit!"

She needed to be alone for awhile and think. Half an hour later she decided she was tired of thinking and took her wine and pretzels out back.

Peg and Jake introduced Joan and Timothy. "They were recently married in Delta Junction, Alaska." Peg said with a chuckle. "They have quite a story to tell, we were waiting till everyone came so they only had to tell the story once."

Looking at her husband, Joan volunteered to tell about her wedding.

"Well," she began; "this is a second marriage for Tim and me. We were married before and that wedding ceremony was very beautiful. We had three children together, and then divorced.

Tim and I got together again a year ago and became engaged in March. Deciding to do a road trip, we took off on a motorcycle. When we reached Delta Junction in Alaska, Tim and I decided to find a Judge, cut out all the fluff and just have a simple wedding. But this wedding turned out to be unusual and special. We found the Judge at City Hall. He was a young man holding court in a blue warehouse type building. We talked to him and he agreed to marry us, but not without two witnesses. We didn't know anyone, but we weren't about to give up our wedding plans either. Walking outside, I saw there was a tour bus across the highway at the visitor's center. People were milling around outside, I could tell they were getting ready to leave. So I hurried over. I talked to a young woman, told her about our dilemma, and she said I'd have to ask the tour director. She led me over to her and I explained that we needed two witnesses to get married."

She looked like she was sizing me up, and then called to the group, "Get on the bus, we're going to a wedding."

I was laughing and crying. The group looked a little puzzled, but she just said, "Come on were going to a wedding."

"We all boarded the bus, I sat in the front. The tour director went to the back of the bus and came back with a bottle of non-alcoholic wine and gave it to me as a wedding gift. The driver drove us across the street and parked the bus we all got off.

When the tour director saw the size of the city hall, she said, "I guess were having an outdoor wedding." And we did!

"The Judge put on his black robe, we lined up in front of the building. The driver was Tim's best man and the tour director was the maid of honor. It was so emotional. Wedding pictures were taken by the woman I originally talked to, she used her phone, then emailed them to us."

Joan continued. "I was crying, happy tears. Tim was crying. I hope happy tears." She said looking at Tim and smiling. "People in the group were wiping their eyes."

Then Tim added, "When the Judge pronounced us man and wife, the group clapped, cheered, laughed, and we got tons of hugs and lots of hand shaking congratulations."

"Anyway," Joan went on, "The certificate was signed, the gold seal was affixed and here we are, married again."

Now the people in the park clapped and cheered, gave hugs, and congratulatory hand shakes.

Jake walked over to the table and begin popping the champagne corks and pouring everyone a drink in clear plastic glasses.

Rusty sat back in the Adirondack chair and smiled. Taking a sip of her bubbly, she knew that everything was going to be just fine.

She'd be going out to see Max soon, and fill him in about Booga and the men who had set up shop at Fred's farm. But that could wait.

Chapter 15

That night Rusty tossed and turned and when she finally slept, she dreamed of William. Waking she noted the alarm clock showed 4:34 AM. Groaning she turned on her back and stared at the dark sky through the skylight. It must be cloudy being she couldn't see the stars. She thought about William and how they met. It was because of him she was living in this tiny house.

William had come into Sandy Bay ahead of a construction crew six years ago. They met at a town hall meeting. The city council was getting the people together to decide if they had a need for tiny houses in the community and if so where this district should be built. William spoke to the townspeople about the advantages of having such a neighborhood. Rusty was impressed with his knowledge of the area and the Scandinavian people who called it home. She was certainly interested in having a place she could call her own. After spending a year in a studio apartment above the *Scissors N' Razor's* hair salon, she knew she could live comfortably in a tiny home. It sounded like something she could afford. She stayed after the meeting to ask questions. At that time she worked as a receptionist for the Medical Center in Plains, twenty miles to the north of Sandy Bay. Housing in Plains was out of her price range so she opted to drive.

The council decided to go ahead with the project and chose the site across the lake from the camp ground. William came back the following month with floor plans and those interested could choose a design and size no larger than 250 square feet. The local bank was at the meeting with information on financing and to make a long story short, Rusty became the owner of a tiny home.

Before William left town, he asked her to dinner, and they exchanged cell phone numbers. The construction crew arrived and began building ten tiny houses. William came into town periodically to check on the progress. Soon he and Rusty became a couple, doing dinner with friends, going to movies, and hanging out at the lake.

Then he moved in with Rusty. It was a whirl wind courtship and in less than a year they were married in a simple wedding. But his job kept him on the road and Rusty continued to work at the Medical Center.

It was William who encouraged her to buy her small shop. He even helped her get a loan with the same banker who mortgaged her house. It wasn't hard to find local vendors who wanted to sell their unique handmade gifts. When word got out about someone opening a craft, gift and wine shop, the artists were bringing in samples. The Hendrix Vineyards were making wine, Jack had a pile of shelves, birdhouses and chests; neither had anywhere to sell them. She was busy trying to clean, paint and put up shelves, when

Nona came into the shop wondering if she needed help. Rusty hired her on the spot. She had been so busy she hardly had time to talk to William

As Rusty lay in her bed, looking through the skylight at the dark night, it was like she was sucked into a hole spiraling down into the past. Her mind whirled her back in time to when her life changed again.

It was a Friday night when the construction crew loaded up their tools and headed out of town. The landscapers put the finishing touches on the walkways and back yards. The pergola was built; small bushes and trees were planted in strategic places. Rusty and William moved into her tiny home. They celebrated with a romantic dinner and drinks at the night club in Plains.

The following morning was a Saturday, William made waffles for Rusty and they lingered over coffee. He decided to rent a boat and go out on the lake to see what he could catch.

Remembering how odd it had seemed to her at the time. She didn't know he liked to fish. But then there was a lot she didn't know about her husband. In fact she never did learn because he died. Correcting her thoughts, he pretended to die.

Rusty had taken the laundry and grocery list to Plains. When she returned Booga and a police officer she didn't know was waiting for her. The boat William had rented that morning had been found floating empty in the middle of the lake. The tackle box, life jacket, and his lunch were in the boat. William was gone! She had to go with the officers to identify his things. Williams name was on the black lunch box, but they still had to be sure. She recognized the boat as belonging to the park and his jacket that was lying across the seat. They began dragging the lake. Nona joined Rusty; they stayed by the lake shore into the night until the men quit searching and then Nona walked her home.

Nona heated up some soup and made her a sandwich, but she wasn't hungry. How could William fall out of his boat? He could swim, why did he drown? She didn't understand.

Lying in her bed, she couldn't remember how she felt. She blocked it out! There were hugs from friends and a memorial service a couple weeks later. Now he was alive! She had to see him.

Being she couldn't sleep she got up, put on her robe, and went downstairs. Rusty made some toast and coffee then carried it out onto the deck to eat. It was just getting light and the night chill was still in the air.

She went to the shop early and Nona came in shortly after, she couldn't sleep either.

"Aren't we a sorry looking couple?" Nona grunted filling the coffee pot with water.

"I'm going to go see him." Rusty said defensively. "I want an explanation."

"Are you sure that is smart?" Nona asked.

"I don't know, and I don't care, I need to confront him."

"When are you going?"

Rusty glanced at the clock and noted it was 8:30 AM, "I think I'll go now!"

Nona raised both her eyebrows and just answered, "Okay."

Rusty nervously puttered around, organizing and refolding some kitchen towels and pot holders. "I am going now!" She exclaimed.

"Okay." Nona repeated.

Rusty looked at the clock, "Do you think I should go now?" It was ten o'clock.

"Go, go for crying out loud, and go!"

"I'm going." Rusty shouted as she banged out the back door and got in her car.

Thirty minutes later Rusty opened the door of the police station. She saw another door propped open, with officer sitting at the desk talking on the phone. Noting the room she was standing in had a vacant desk in the corner with empty chairs lining the wall, she sat down in one while she waited. Soon the officer came to the door.

"Can I help you?" he asked.

"I came to see one of your inmates, his name is William, or Benjamin, or maybe Conrad. He came in last night."

"Guess I know who you want to see. He's not eligible for bail." The officer replied.

"I'm not bailing him out; I need to talk to him."

"Who are you? Why do you need to see him?"

Rusty replied, "I'm his ex wife, or one of them, I need to see him."

The officer studied her, then said, "I guess, it would be okay, I'll need to ask you to leave your purse here, and have you empty your pockets. I'll have someone get him and you can talk in the interrogation room."

The officer went back to the desk and picked up the phone. Rusty set her purse on his desk and took the cell phone out of her pocket and laid that down.

"Come with me," the officer instructed.

She followed him through another door into a hall way. The room where he led her to was at the end of the hall, it was empty except for two chairs and a table. She paced while she waited. A police guard ushered William into the room and to a chair by the table.

"I'll be just outside the door," He informed her before leaving the room.

William looked surprised when he saw her, and she noted that he was getting grey, he looked thinner, but his eyes were still a striking blue. She didn't say anything. When the officer left William got up, his hands were cuffed, and he held them at his chest as he walked toward her. She didn't move just looked into his eyes. When he was close enough she doubled her fist and hit him as hard as she could in the groin. As he doubled over, she took the flat of her hand and slapped him under the nose, pushing his head back until she could feel the cartilage give way.

At the door she turned and looked at him again. The blood was gushing from his nose onto the floor, his eyes were watering.

Rusty walked down the hall, stopping at the desk to pick up her purse and phone she said to the officer.

"You should maybe check on him, he may need a doctor." She smiled and said, "You have a good day now and thanks."

Walking to her car, she felt a weight lift off her shoulders, and said out loud. "I just love being me! Maybe I will get a dog, just a little one."